Communications in Computer and Information Science　　1339

More information about this series at http://www.springer.com/series/7899

Hein Venter · Marianne Loock ·
Marijke Coetzee · Mariki Eloff ·
Jan Eloff · Reinhardt Botha (Eds.)

Information
and Cyber Security

19th International Conference, ISSA 2020
Pretoria, South Africa, August 25–26, 2020
Revised Selected Papers

 Springer

Editors
Hein Venter (iD)
University of Pretoria
Pretoria, South Africa

Marijke Coetzee (iD)
University of Johannesburg
Auckland Park, South Africa

Jan Eloff (iD)
University of Pretoria
Pretoria, South Africa

Marianne Loock (iD)
University of South Africa
Florida, South Africa

Mariki Eloff (iD)
University of South Africa
Pretoria, South Africa

Reinhardt Botha (iD)
Nelson Mandela University
Port Elizabeth, South Africa

ISSN 1865-0929   ISSN 1865-0937   (electronic)
Communications in Computer and Information Science
ISBN 978-3-030-66038-3   ISBN 978-3-030-66039-0   (eBook)
https://doi.org/10.1007/978-3-030-66039-0

This Springer imprint is published by the registered company Springer Nature Switzerland AG
The registered company address is: Gewerbestrasse 11, 6330 Cham, Switzerland

Preface

ISSA 2020 is the annual conference for the information security community that continues on the successful recipe established in 2001. The conference is held under the auspices of the Academy for Computer Science and Software Engineering at the University of Johannesburg, South Africa, the School of Computing at the University of South Africa, and the Department of Computer Science at the University of Pretoria, South Africa.

The ISSA 2020 conference was held during August 25–26, 2020. The conference has evolved each year in various ways. For the first time the conference was hosted online due to the COVID-19 worldwide pandemic. However, that did not hold us back to still host a fantastic online conference. We believe that the quality and relevance of the information presented by industry practitioners and academics have also evolved over the years. This year university students and other non-presenting delegates were allowed to register for the conference at no cost. A record virtual attendance of almost 200 delegates was recorded!

Conferences have become a major focus area – and often a money spinner – in many industries, so at any time a number of conferences were being advertised in similar fields such as information or cyber security. What sets the ISSA conference apart is that it is not intended to generate a profit for an organization, and it does not encourage marketing of products and services through presentations. Instead, the proceeds from registration fees are reinvested to ensure that the conference evolves each year. This year, due to the virtual nature of the conference, minimal costs were incurred. Sponsors are afforded an opportunity to present company-specific information that has a bearing on the conference themes, and presentations submitted by potential speakers are sent through a vigorous double-blind review process, managed by a team of respected international experts in information security.

We trust that the annual ISSA conference will continue to be recognized as a plat-form for professionals from industry as well as researchers to share their knowledge, experience, and research results in the field of information and cyber security not only on a South African level, but also on an international one.

To ensure ongoing improvement, every year we encourage input from all those interested in the field of information and cyber security, particularly those who are actively seeking to progress the field, to take part and share their knowledge and experience.

August 2020

Hein Venter
Marianne Loock
Marijke Coetzee
Mariki Eloff
Jan Eloff
Reinhardt Botha

Conference Focus

Information security has evolved and in the last few years there has been renewed interest in the subject worldwide. This is evident from the many standards and certifications now available to guide security strategy. This has led to a clearer career path for security professionals.

The Internet of Things (IoT) together with advances in wireless communications, have brought new security challenges for the information security fraternity. As these IoT devices become more available, and more organizations attempt to rid their offices of "spaghetti," the protection of data in these environments becomes a more important consideration. It is this fraternity that organizations, governments, and communities in general look to for guidance on best practice in this converging world.

Identity theft and phishing are ongoing concerns. What we are now finding is that security mechanisms have become so good and are generally implemented by companies wanting to adhere to good corporate governance, attackers are now looking to the weak link in the chain, namely the individual user. It is far easier to attack them than attempt to penetrate sophisticated and secure corporate systems. A spate of ransomware is also doing the rounds, with waves of malware still striking periodically. Software suppliers have started stepping up to protect their users and take some responsibility for security in general and not just for their own products.

The conference therefore focused on all aspects of information and cyber security and invited participation across the information security spectrum, including but not limited to, functional, business, managerial, theoretical, and technological issues.

Invited speakers talked about the international trends in information security products, methodologies, and management issues, specifically in dealing with security during the COVID-19 pandemic. In the past ISSA has secured many highly acclaimed international speakers, including:

- Pieter Geldenhuys, Vice-chair of the Innovation Focus Group at the International Communications Union, Switzerland. Topic: BUSINESS UNUSUAL: Strategic insight in creating the future. Leveraging the value of the Hyper-connected world.
- Wayne Kearney, Manager: Risk & Assurance at Water Corporation, Australia. Topic: Why are management shocked with all the "PHISH" caught? A case study in perspective.
- Prof. Dr. Sylvia Osborn, Associate Professor of Computer Science, University of Western Ontario, Canada. Topic: Role-based access control: is it still relevant?
- Prof. Dr. Steve Marsh, Associate Professor at the Ontario Tech University, Canada. Topic: Trust and Security - Links, Relationships, and Family Feuds.
- Alice Sturgeon manages the area that is accountable for identifying and architecting horizontal requirements across the Government of Canada. Her topic made reference to An Identity Management Architecture for the Government of Canada.
- Dr. Alf Zugenmaier, DoCoMo Lab, Germany. His topic was based on Security and Privacy.

- William List, WM List and Co., UK. His topic was: Beyond the Seventh Layer live the users.
- Prof. Dennis Longley, Queensland University of Technology, Australia. His topic was: IS Governance: Will it be effective?
- Prof. TC Ting: University of Connecticut, and fellow of the Computing Research Association, USA.
- Prof. Dr. Stephanie Teufel: Director of the International Institute of Management in Telecommunications (iimt). Fribourg University, Switzerland.
- Rich Schiesser, Senior Technical Planner at Option One Mortgage, USA; Rick Cudworth, Partner, KPMG LLP, International Service Leader, Security and Business Continuity - Europe, Middle East, and Africa.
- Dario Forte - CISM, CFE, Founder, DFLabs, and Adj. Faculty University of Milan, Italy.
- Reijo Savola - Network and information security research coordinator, VTT Technical Research Centre of Finland, Finland.
- Mark Pollitt - Ex Special Agent of the Federal Bureau of Investigation (FBI) and professor at the Daytona State College, USA.
- Prof Joachim Biskup - Professor of Computer Science, Technische Universität Dortmund, Germany.
- Dr Andreas Schaad - Research Program Manager, SAP Research Security & Trust Group, Germany.
- Prof Steven Furnell - Head of School of Computing, Electronics and Mathematics at the University of Plymouth, UK.
- Prof Matt Warren - School of Information and Business Analytics, Deakin University, Australia.
- Christian Damsgaard Jensen - Associate Professor, Institute for Mathematics and Computer Science, Technical University of Denmark, Denmark.
- Prof Rebecca Wright - Director of DIMACS, Rutgers University, USA.

The purpose of the conference was to provide information security practitioners and researchers worldwide with the opportunity to share their knowledge and research results with their peers. The objectives of the conference are defined as follows:

- Sharing of knowledge, experience, and best practice
- Promoting networking and business opportunities
- Encouraging the research and study of information security
- Supporting the development of a professional information security community
- Assisting self-development
- Providing a forum for education, knowledge transfer, professional development, and development of new skills
- Promoting best practice in information security and its application in Southern Africa
- Facilitating the meeting of diverse cultures to share and learn from each other in the quest for safer information systems

Organization

Conference General Chairs

Hein Venter	University of Pretoria, South Africa
Marijke Coetzee	University of Johannesburg, South Africa
Marianne Loock	University of South Africa, South Africa
Mariki Eloff	University of South Africa, South Africa
Jan Eloff	University of Pretoria, South Africa

Organizing Committee

Mariki Eloff	University of South Africa, South Africa
Marijke Coetzee	University of Johannesburg, South Africa
Marianne Loock	University of South Africa, South Africa
Hein Venter	University of Pretoria, South Africa
Jan Eloff	University of Pretoria, South Africa

Program Committee

Reinhardt Botha	Nelson Mandela University, South Africa
Marianne Loock	University of South Africa, South Africa
Mariki Eloff	University of South Africa, South Africa

Publication Chair

Hein Venter	University of Pretoria, South Africa

Honorary Committee

The following member is an honorary committee member of the ISSA conference. This committee member is honored for his effort as one of the founding members of the ISSA conference in 2001. The current conference committee feels obliged to honor him as such.

Les Labuschagne	University of South Africa, South Africa

On behalf of the general conference chairs, we would like to extend our heartfelt appreciation to all the conference committee members and chairs for their hard work in organizing ISSA 2020! Without your continuous hard work and efforts, ISSA 2020 would not have been possible. Again, we thank you!

Review Committee

A rigorous double-blind refereeing process was undertaken by an international panel of referees to ensure the quality of submissions before acceptance. Authors initially submit abstracts to determine if the paper meets the goals and fits into the theme of the conference. The ISSA Program Committee assesses each submission for relevance and fit. Authors are then notified whether their abstracts were accepted, and if so, invited to submit a full paper for peer review. The task of a reviewer is often a thankless task, however, without them this conference would not be possible. The ISSA Organizing Committee would like to extend their heartfelt thanks to the list of reviewers below, whom include leading information security experts from around the world.

On the due date, authors submit full papers, anonymized by the authors for the double-blind review process. Each paper goes through an administrative review and is assigned to at least three reviewers selected from an international panel of reviewers, in order to confirm that the paper conforms to the specifications and quality for the conference. If a paper does not meet the requirements, the author is asked to make the required changes as indicated by reviewers and asked to resubmit the paper, or to consider submitting the paper to another conference.

A review committee is invited to participate, consisting of both local and international experts in the field of information security. A process is followed by the Program Committee to allocate papers to reviewers based on their area of expertise. Reviewers are subject matter experts, of which over 50% are international. Reviewers usually have 5 or 6 categories that they are willing to review against. Each reviewer will establish the number of papers they can review in a specific time period and are allowed to bid on the papers they want to review. An automated process allocated papers to each reviewer according to their preferences.

Each paper is reviewed by a minimum of two reviewers (but mostly by three reviewers) in a double-blind review process. Papers are reviewed and rated on a 5 point system with 1 being poor and 5 being excellent as follows:

- Originality (1 to 5)
- Contribution (1 to 5)
- Overall quality (1 to 5)
- Reviewer's confidence (1 to 5)
- Overall evaluation (calculated by an algorithm as a number in the range −5 to 5, where a negative score of −5 would indicate an extremely strong reject, 0 would indicate a borderline paper and 5 would indicate an extremely strong accept)

Reviewers' confidence in their own rating is also taken into account by the algorithm that calculates the overall evaluation. Reviewers are also encouraged to make anonymous suggestions to the author(s) of the paper.

Based on the overall evaluation (−5 to 5), a paper with 0 or below points can be recommended for a poster/research-in-progress session and a 3 to 5 point paper can be put in the "best paper" category. An acceptance rate of between 25% and 35% is maintained for the conference. In 2020 the acceptance rate was 30%.

Authors are notified of the outcome of the review process, which includes the anonymous suggestions and recommendations of the reviewers. Authors then have to submit the final version of the paper that will then be included in the formal conference proceedings. This proceedings is the official version of the proceedings. An unofficial version of the proceedings was distributed during the conference. All unofficial proceedings from all previous ISSA conferences are also available at https://www.infosecsa.com/past-proceedings.

Name	Company/Affiliation	Country	
Hanifa Abdullah	University of South Africa	South Africa	
Richard Ikuesan	Community College Qatar	Qatar	
Alapan Arnab	Private	South Africa	
Sampson Asare	University of Botswana	Botswana	
Frans Blauw	University of Johannesburg	South Africa	
KP Chow	The University of Hong Kong	Hong Kong	
Deon Cotterell	University of Johannesburg	South Africa	
Evan Dembsky	University of South Africa	South Africa	
Moses Dlamini	University of Pretoria	South Africa	
Lynette Drevin	North-West University	South Africa	
Jaco du Toit	University of Johannesburg	South Africa	
Eduardo Fernandez	Florida Atlantic University	USA	
Stephen Flowerday	University of Fort Hare	South Africa	
Evangelos Frangopoulos	University of South Africa	Greece	
Steven Furnell	University of Plymouth	UK	
Lynn Futcher	Nelson Mandela Metropolitan University	South Africa	
Indren Govender	Stellenbosch University	South Africa	
Brian Greaves	University of Johannesburg	South Africa	

(*Continued*)

(Continued)

Name	Company/Affiliation	Country	
Stefanos Gritzalis	University of the Aegean	Greece	
Paul Haskell-Dowland	Edith Cowan University	Australia	
Bertram Haskins	Nelson Mandela University	South Africa	
Barry Irwin	Rhodes University	South Africa	
Christian Damsgaard Jensen	Technical University of Denmark	Denmark	
Jason Jordaan	DFIR Labs	South Africa	
Nickson Karie	Edith Cowan University	Australia	
Victor Kebande	Malmö University	Sweden	
Hennie Kruger	North-West University	South Africa	
Grace Leung	University of Johannesburg	South Africa	
Candice Louw	University of Johannesburg	South Africa	
Buks Louwrens	Quintessence Digital Forensics	South Africa	
Mathias Mujinga	University of Pretoria	South Africa	
Martin Olivier	University of Pretoria	South Africa	
Rolf Oppliger	eSECURITY Technologies	Switzerland	
Jacques Ophoff	University of Cape Town	South Africa	
Mauricio Papa	The University of Tulsa	USA	
Guenther Pernul	University of Regensburg	Germany	
Rayne Reid	Nelson Mandela Metropolitan University	South Africa	
Karen Renaud	The University of Glasgow	UK	
George Sibiya	CSIR	South Africa	
Stephanie Teufel	University of Fribourg	Switzerland	

(Continued)

(*Continued*)

Name	Company/Affiliation	Country	
Aleksandar Valjarevic	Vlatacom Research and Development Institute	Serbia	
Maureen van Den Bergh	University of Johannesburg	South Africa	
Carl van der Westhuizen	University of Johannesburg	South Africa	
Brett van Niekerk	University of Kwazulu Natal	South Africa	
Alf Zugenmaier	Munich University of Applied Sciences	Germany	
Wynand van Staden	University of South Arica	South Africa	

Contents

Risks and Threats Arising from the Adoption of Digital Technology
in Treasury.. 1
    Johan von Solms and Josef Langerman

Cyber Security Canvas for SMEs 20
    Stephanie Teufel, Bernd Teufel, Mohammad Aldabbas,
    and Minh Nguyen

Risk Forecasting Automation on the Basis of MEHARI................ 34
    Pavel Yermalovich and Mohamed Mejri

Protecting Personal Data Within a South African Organisation 50
    Mitesh Singh, Colin Pilkington, and Wynand van Staden

Concern for Information Privacy in South Africa: An Empirical Study
Using the OIPCI.. 65
    Adéle da Veiga

Security Education, Training, and Awareness: Incorporating a Social
Marketing Approach for Behavioural Change 81
    Moneer Alshaikh, Sean B. Maynard, and Atif Ahmad

Exploring Emotion Detection as a Possible Aid in Speaker Authentication... 96
    Ebenhaeser Otto Janse van Rensburg, Reinhardt A. Botha,
    and Rossouw Von Solms

Identification of Information Security Controls for Fitness
Wearable Manufacturers....................................... 112
    Sophia Moganedi and Dalenca Pottas

A Critical Evaluation of Validation Practices in the Forensic Acquisition
of Digital Evidence in South Africa............................. 129
    Jason Jordaan and Karen Bradshaw

Investigating Customer-Facing Security Features on South
African E-commerce Websites 144
    Deen Brandreth and Jacques Ophoff

Author Index 161

Risks and Threats Arising from the Adoption of Digital Technology in Treasury

Johan von Solms[(✉)] and Josef Langerman

University of Johannesburg, Johannesburg, South Africa
jvonsolms@gmail.com, josef.langerman@standardbank.co.za

Abstract. The importance of Treasury management, within a commercial bank has increased significantly over the last couple of years. After the 2008 financial crisis the role and responsibility of a Treasury department has changed in terms of scope and strategic importance, evolving from a transactional cash manager to the guardian of the balance sheet. In order to meet this broader strategic mandate, Treasurers must therefore consider ways to become more effective and streamlined, while reducing time-consuming operational activities. Digitalisation can address many of the traditional Treasury challenges and provide a number of commercial and competitive benefits as well. However, to successfully adopt digital technologies and related digital innovations, Treasury requires a well-defined digital transformation plan. The Smart Digital Treasury Model (SDTM) was developed to provide a comprehensive roadmap to assist a Treasury's digital transition towards a next generation 'smart' Treasury department. This paper explores a key building block of the SDTM, which addresses the risks and threats that can arise from the adoption of new digital technology. The reason for focusing on this aspect is that many of the digital risks have no direct reference points with conventional banking activity or security measures. The result of this research is an approach that articulates Treasury specific digital risks and threats, as well as describes a risk management process that can be deployed as part of the digital transformation. The digital landscape is evolving the whole time; therefore, digital risk management activity in Treasury can't be seen as a once-off exercise, but needs to evolve in line with market developments.

Keywords: Digital technology · Digitalisation · Innovation · Smart treasury · Digital risks and threats · Evolution of treasury · Cyber security

1 Introduction

The Treasury department in a commercial bank plays a crucial role in managing a commercial bank's scarce financial resources such as capital and liquidity. The responsibility of the Treasury department has changed significantly over the last couple of decades and especially since the 2008 financial crisis. During this time, Treasury has evolved from being primarily focussed on transactional activities such as cash management to becoming the guardian of the holistic balance sheet, with an important role in setting the firm's strategic direction.

© Springer Nature Switzerland AG 2020
H. Venter et al. (Eds.): ISSA 2020, CCIS 1339, pp. 1–19, 2020.
https://doi.org/10.1007/978-3-030-66039-0_1

These changes in the Treasury mandate were driven by a combination of factors, including developments in regulations, technology, monetary policy and the altering of the competitive landscape. As the custodian of the balance sheet and manager of scarce and expensive financial resources, Treasury is under ongoing pressure on various fronts and therefore requires change and transformation to remain effective. On the one side, the regulatory requirements are becoming more onerous calling for greater granularity and precision, higher frequency of reporting and forward-looking analytical capabilities. On the other side, the Chief Executive Officer or Chief Financial Officer increasingly looks to the Treasurer, often in real-time, for strategic decision-making and holistic attestation that the balance sheet is efficiently optimised.

For many Treasury departments there are a number of obstacles in the way of achieving this broader strategic mandate, including: the complexity of a bank's business model, fragmentation of upstream systems, legacy technology not tailored for evolving Treasury needs and large amounts of data to process and analyse. Comprehensive digitalisation of Treasury can help address some of these challenges and can deliver a range of commercial benefits, for example: reduce operating costs, enhance Net Interest Income, improve risk management and optimisation of capital and liquidity buffers [17].

Leveraging appropriate digital technology solutions for core activities like risk management of Liquidity and Capital - which requires large amounts of data analysis, real-time decisions, and complex forecasting - can provide a number of advantages for Treasury. These benefits include:

- Deliver on its growing strategic mandate by automating manual processes to reduce operational activities and support better strategic decision making;
- Keep tread with digital transformation in the rest of the bank, which will increasingly put pressure on Treasury's legacy systems and processes, if no corresponding digital transformation takes place;
- Ensure an ongoing competitive advantage relative to developments in challenger banks and Fintech competitors; and
- Future proof Treasury against anticipated step changes in the financial markets for example open banking.

A problem is that Treasury tends to be a slow adopter of digital technology and often does not have a well-articulated digital strategy. A survey by the Boston Consulting Group of 44 banks revealed that most Treasury functions have relatively low level of digital maturity. The analysis shows that only 11pct of bank Treasuries made widespread use of advanced technologies and use cases, while about 70pct have yet to embrace digitalisation in any meaningful way [14]. The 2019 PWC Global Treasury benchmarking survey [12], found that the biggest roadblocks for implementing digital technologies in Treasury were inter-alia:

- lack of digital use cases/business cases;
- no mid to long term strategy; and
- lack of people skills.

There is thus a requirement for a Treasury specific digital transformation model which provides clear guidance for its digital transformation journey. The Smart Digital Treasury Model (SDTM) was previously developed with the objective to provide a Treasury a well-defined roadmap, in the transition towards becoming a more mature digital user. The logic and approach of the SDTM was researched and described by the authors in a prior paper [32] and comprises of four main building blocks namely:

1. Digital Maturity Assessment and identification of digital use cases;
2. Digital Technology evaluation and Business Case development;
3. Technology implementation plan; and
4. Management of Digital Technology Risks and Threats.

This paper will focus on the fourth building block of the SDTM, namely the identification and management of risks and threats that can arise in Treasury due to the adoption of new digital technology.

Section 2 looks at a literature review and the reasons why it is critical to identify, consider and mitigate any exposures that may arise as part of the digital transition of a Treasury. Section 3 briefly introduces the Smart Digital Treasury Model (SDTM) and describes its different building blocks. Section 4 explains the different risks and threats that a Treasury might face when adopting new digital technologies. Section 5 considers a holistic risk management solution to combat the new digital exposures.

2 Literature Review

A bank's Treasury department has evolved significantly over the last couple of decades [3]. The discipline has its roots in the latter part of the previous century, with the introduction of Treasury specific management systems and software. Over the turn of the century many Treasury functions turned from a regional focus to a more global focus as banks consolidated and expanded internationally [23]. However, since the 2008 financial crisis, Treasury's role and responsibility has changed significantly. The evolution can be divided into distinct stages, driven by the developments in regulations [26], new technology [8], monetary policy [27] and competitor activity [16]. The high-level stages are:

Pre the Financial Crisis (prior to 2008) no comprehensive global regulations were enforced for certain key risks such liquidity and balance sheet leverage. One of the outcomes were that funding were readily available and relatively cheap and the Cost of Funds was therefore not accurately reflected in new asset origination, resulting in an increase in credit supply and low loan margins - with limited leeway to absorb future funding shocks [25]. Therefore, when the 2008 financial crisis hit, banks struggled to continue financing their bulky balance sheets on a profitable basis.

Post the Financial Crisis (2008 to 2015) a range of new regulations were introduced (i.e. Basel III accord, Dodd-Frank and others) calling for higher capital buffers, larger liquid asset portfolios, more granular and frequent reporting, stress testing etc. [28]. In order to meet these increasing prudential demands and ensure the regulations were implemented, different Treasury related activities [6] were centralised into a Group Treasury unit [24].

The new Regulatory regime (after c. 2015) meant the role of Treasury started to shift more towards becoming a guardian of the balance sheet, with responsibility for the holistic management of all assets and liabilities. One reason was that senior management needed to ensure the balance sheet was sustainable and profitable going forward, in light of all the prudential constraints that was imposed on scarce balance sheet resources like capital and liquidity.

In order to meet this broader strategic mandate Treasury must consider different technology solutions such as digitalisation to become more efficient and streamlined by reducing time-consuming operational activities. The problem is that Treasury management is increasingly faced with the difficult challenge of weighing the value of deploying new digital solutions to improve internal processes and ward of external competitors against the potential new risks that the technology potentially creates. The reality is that new technology often equals new risks. A 'tried and tested' technology infrastructure has a known risk profile; however, deploying cutting edge innovation creates a different kind of risk profile and therefore new technology is often far more vulnerable.

As an example, Volt a new online bank in Australia is one of first banks globally, that will perform all its processing and data storage in the cloud [20]. This approach has significant benefits compared to using old legacy banking systems, but comes with a totally new set of risks and exposures, which needs to be managed.

This increased risk is especially relevant for traditional Treasury functions which is used to operating in a centralised environment, where data and its activities are protected behind the external firewalls and security measures of the broader bank's defences. These risks have made many regulators hesitant to open the distributed computing field too rapidly. In a recent report the Bank of England indicated that it has ongoing concerns about 'concentration risk and lack of substitutability', pointing to lingering worries about the wisdom of putting critical financial applications on someone else's infrastructure, which has not been immune to resilience issues [30].

This reservation is also shared in some regard by market participants. In 2018 the Association of Finance Professionals (AFP) undertook a risk survey, where they found that Treasury and finance professionals are worried about emerging technologies even as those technologies provides increasing benefits [1]. The following findings were made:

- A majority of survey respondents cited Artificial Intelligence, Robotic Process Automation and Data Engineering as technologies that could expose their companies to additional risks;
- Treasury and finance professionals perceive new technology risks through a traditional cybersecurity lens. However, operational risks and business continuity risks are also cited as consequences from the introduction of new technologies;
- A majority of organizations has no Board approved risk-appetite policy;
- One third of organizations are unprepared for new risks arising from the implementation of new technology and only a small percentage are confident in their preparations.

It is therefore crucial that as part of the digital transformation journey of a Treasury function, all the potentially digital risks are identified and plans are put in place to address these additional threats. The European Banking Authority (EBA) published a report in

January 2020 on the impact of Big Data and Advanced Analytics [13]. It found that a data-driven approach is emerging across the banking sector, affecting bank's business strategies, risk, technology and operations. The report notes a number of fundamental challenges that needs to be sufficiently addressed. These risk factors include: Ethics, Explainability and Interpretability, Fairness and Avoidance of bias, Traceability and Auditability, Data protection, Data quality, and Security and Consumer protection. The AFP Risk survey [1] found that new or increased risks being managed as a result of increased digital technology are: Cyber Security, Operational Risk, Business Continuation, Error and omissions, Regulatory Risk, Cloud Risk, Reputational Risk and People Risk.

Since all these risk factors can have an influence on a Treasury department when it adopts new digital technology, it is crucial to study them in more detail. The reason is that Treasury is a significant user of data in order to interpret information for strategic capital and liquidity decision making purposes, leaving it exposed to arising digital threats. Academic literature often overlaps in terms of the main digital risks and concerns and importantly tends not to be Treasury specific. Therefore, this paper will study the risks and threats that can arise and requires attention in the context of a Treasury's digital transformation.

The research methodology underpinning this study takes the form of a Design Science research. The reason is that a Design Science approach works well for problems that reside at the intersection of Information Technology and deployment thereof in organisations. The digitalisation of a Treasury function fits into this paradigm. The output of the research is to produce an Artefact (i.e. Smart Digital Treasury Model), which will have practical value to both a research and professional audience. The Risks and Threats component explored in this paper forms an integral part of this Artefact.

The next section will briefly introduce the Smart Digital Treasury Model (SDTM) to explain how the management of digital risks and threats fit into the overarching model. Following from that the digital risk and threat elements relevant for a Treasury will be identified and explored in more detail.

3 Smart Treasury Digital Model (STDM)

The emphasis on digital technologies and digital strategy in banks have increased significantly over the last couple of years. The development of digital applications in areas like: online banking, customer payments, credit scoring, fraud prevention and detecting money laundering has grown in leaps and bounds. The common denominator in most of these applications is often the customer interfacing dimension. The rationale is that it simplifies banking for clients, improves customer experience and leads to cost reduction, in that there is a reduced need for bricks and mortar branches.

On the face of it many banks would therefore appear relatively advanced in the adoption of digital technologies or on a pathway to achieve digital maturity in the foreseeable future. However, the progress of digitalisation in a bank is not consistent throughout the organisation. One area specifically that has not kept up with wider digital development is the Treasury department. A recent survey found that most Treasury professionals (97pct) still use Excel as their primary tool, ironically while 28pct believes it is not a fit for purpose risk management tool [1].

Given the growing importance of bank Treasuries and its increasing strategic management mandate many departments, in line with the broader developments in banking, are looking at digital solutions to manage its activities more effectively. To achieve this objective, it is crucial to have a Treasury specific framework in place to measure the present digital maturity and provide guidance on the transitioning to a more advanced digital environment. The Smart Digital Treasury Model (SDTM) was developed for this purpose, namely to support and guide the evolution towards a next generation smart Treasury department fit for the 4th Industrial Revolution. In a paper entitled *'A Smart Treasury fit for the 4th Industrial Revolution'* the approach of how the model was designed and developed is described in more detail. In summary the main components that can impact a Treasury's digital transformation was identified and combined into an overarching model [32]. Figure 1 provides more insight on the underlying building blocks of the SDTM.

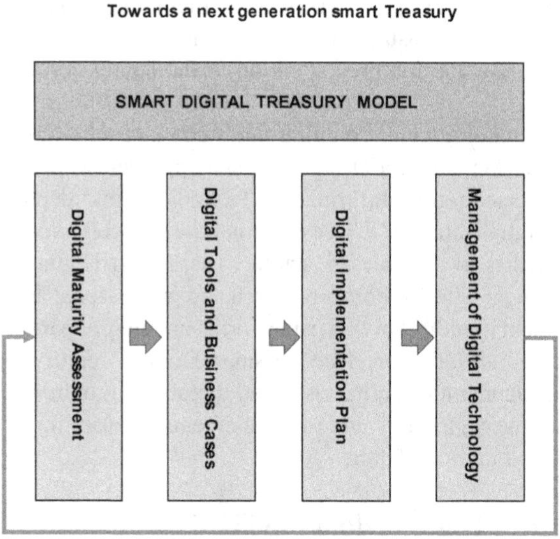

Towards a next generation smart Treasury

Fig. 1. Smart Digital Treasury Model (SDTM)

The model comprises of four building blocks:

- **Block 1: Digital Maturity Assessment and Identification of Digital Use Cases** - measures the digital maturity of a Treasury against a specific set of criteria and scores the digitalisation level/readiness on a scale from beginner to advanced. It then identifies and describes digital use cases for the core Treasury activities and rank these for further development.
- **Block 2: Digital Technology Evaluation and Business Case Development** - digital use cases are mapped into the most appropriate digital technology tools. It is then build-out into more detailed business cases, that are prioritised based on defined requirements as well as performance hurdles like Return on Investment (ROI). This is

to ensure that any subsequent implementation will deliver the expected benefits and ensure the Treasury transition successfully to a more digitally mature state.

- **Block 3: Digital road map of Technology implementation** - this building block articulates the execution plan and approach applied to implement the new digital technology.
- **Block 4: Management of risks originating from Digital Technology adoption** - managing the risks and increased threats arising from digitalisation in Treasury is an important consideration. It therefore requires a dedicated approach to identify and mitigate these potential risks.

The contribution of the model is that it provides a unified and comprehensive approach, specifically to assist a commercial bank's Treasury department in its digital transformation. The adoption of digital technology can be a difficult and expensive endeavour. It is therefore imperative that a Treasury department has a well-articulated plan or roadmap in place that can guide its transition towards a smart function in an effective manner. For example, one of the key building blocks at the start of the digital journey is to perform a Digital Maturity Assessment. Von Solms [31] describes how a Digital Maturity Assessment (DMA) can be implemented specifically for a Treasury, that measures its existing digital maturity level and identify the gaps to focus on for future digitalisation.

The SDTM ensures that the subsequent digital technology evaluation and implementation thereof is done in an integrated manner. Also, that there are a pro-active awareness and focus on digital risks and threats through-out the adoption process, rather than as an after-thought once the technology has been deployed. This next section will focus on the fourth building block of the SDTM, namely the management of risks and threats that may arise due to the adoption of new digital technology.

4   Identifying Risks and Threats that May Arise from Adopting Digital Technology

Digital technologies like Artificial Intelligence, Machine Learning, and Advanced Data analytics have existed in some form or shape for the last couple of decades. However, the recent growth in processing power and the explosion of data available to 'learn from' mean innovative analytical tools are becoming far more useful and effective.

An area in the bank that can gain significant advantage from leveraging digital technology is the Treasury function. The reason is that there are a number of its activities, which fits well into a digital technology framework e.g. cash flow forecasting can be improved by Machine Learning; Payments and settlements can be automated through Artificial Intelligence; while Risk Management and Reporting of Capital and Liquidity exposures will greatly benefit from Big Data and Advanced analytics.

As a Treasury adopts more of these technologies it is important to identify all of the potential digital risks and how to mitigate them. A systematic search of academic literature finds a number of studies focussing on security awareness and training in general [5] and specifically within the banking domain [10, 22]. There are also a wide range of literature that covers the subject area of threat intelligence and provides policies and frameworks for the effective management in banking [4, 19, 29]. Although all very applicable for a Treasury department a consideration is that many of these are not focussed on Treasury. Another factor is that digital risks can also include more qualitative aspects - such as explainability of model decisions, fairness, regulatory risks - which are also relevant for Treasury activity. For example, the European Banking Association [13] identifies a comprehensive spectrum of potential risk and threats to consider when deploying Big Data, while the Association of Finance Professionals [1] highlights the main risk factors to manage with increased use of digital technology.

This section attempts to evaluate the various risks and threats identified from academic literature into a dedicated Treasury focussed framework. The basis for proposing the following risks were validated through structured interviews with Treasury experts. The key risk factors identified for consideration in a Treasury department is shown below in Fig. 2.

Fig. 2. Risks factors related to adopting digital technology in Treasury

Each of these seven risk factors are discussed in more detail below:

4.1 Risk Driver 1 - Explainability

The use of digital technologies including Machine Learning, Big Data and Advanced Analytics can quickly lead to untransparent 'black box' systems. This can make it very difficult to always understand, the internal behaviour or logic and verify how the model has reached a certain conclusion or result.

Opaque systems stand in direct opposition to explainability. Transparency is about being able to describe, inspect and reproduce the mechanisms through which the digital solution derives an outcome and having the appropriate governance in place. In different terms it means explaining the rules that the algorithm uses in a way that can be easily understood by humans [13].

Lack of explainability represents a serious threat for digitalising a Treasury. The reason is that Treasury is the gatekeeper of the bank's balance sheet and the manager of the scarce resources including capital and liquidity. It therefore has an important fiduciary duty to report and explain these balance sheet constraints to regulators, senior management, businesses and external shareholders in a clear manner. The capital and liquidity numbers can influence a wide range of aspects, from impacting on business growth to raising regulatory concern around the viability and financial robustness of the bank.

When a Treasury adopts digital technology it therefore needs to ensure that all the steps and decisions made through-out the entire analytics process are clear, transparent and traceable to enable oversight. In essence this translates to auditability, which is the ability for an outside entity (e.g. the regulator) to review how Treasury developed its algorithm, without compromising the bank's intellectual property.

4.2   Risk Driver 2 - Cyber Security

Banks as the custodians of money have been under attack for hundreds of years. In the beginning, it was the physical theft of monies from 'brick and mortar' branches. Then it moved to computer fraud using technology. Today, it's not just cyber theft of money, but also the hacking of bank systems to obtain personal information on customers. This is why cyber security in banking is of utmost importance [7]. Treasury has access to a vast amount of bank data because it has links into a wide range of banking systems inter-alia:

- Customer Product systems used for Loan and Deposit Pricing;
- Risk Management systems used for Interest Rate Risk management;
- Trading Systems containing trading strategies; and
- Finance and Accounting systems holding all bank's financial information.

The reason Treasury requires this myriad of data is in order to construct a holistic picture of the balance sheet to manage the funding, liquidity, and capital positions as well as the banking book risks (e.g. interest rate and currency).

Furthermore, it normally integrates this fragmented data and transforms it into valuable management information e.g. capital demand, contingent liquidity requirement and interest rate risk exposure. This management information is used in senior management committees for example the Asset and Liability Committee (ALCO) to support strategic decision making [15]. This centralised and strategic function makes Treasury somewhat unique in the organisation and therefore it has always been open to a range of specific computer security risks e.g.

- Theft of important confidential information like the ALCO report and supporting analysis;

- Hacking into Treasury Management Systems such as the payment and settlement systems to influence payments and/or commit payment fraud; and
- Viruses infecting systems that drives trading decisions and hedging.

Treasury has a number of defensive security measures in place, that are normally aligned with the bank's wider security policy. This can include biometrics, authentication and authorisation, firewalls etc. One of the major defensive techniques for a Treasury is that its data, models and systems are usually on bank owned infrastructure and maintained centrally.

The adoption of more advanced digital technology can impede these traditional protective measures and generate additional risks, normally due to the higher connectivity to the internet. Using distributed cloud computing functionality can open up Treasury to widespread attacks on its sensitive management information. Also, it could involve potential hacking of its 'intelligent' proprietary digital models (i.e. Big Data and Advanced analytical models). This type of model attack could entail model theft (e.g. stealing intellectual knowledge) or model poisoning (e.g. influencing the model's behaviour/output in a known or unknow manner).

It is therefore important for a Treasury to pro-actively enhance and strengthen its security measures as it adopts digital technology. This could include maintaining a technical watch, and regular updates on progress on security attacks and related defence techniques.

4.3   Risk Driver 3 - Fairness and Avoidance of Bias

A number of regulators have raised concerns that digital technology like Artificial Intelligence may unintentionally exclude customers from access to banking if it introduces bias against certain new customers or those seeking loans. For example, the Hong Kong Monetary Authority (HKMA) has put directives in place seeking to ensure customers and their data are treated fairly [18].

Bias can be introduced into the process through either the data or the algorithm being used. In the former, the outcome might be impacted by the way the data is collected or selected for use. In the latter, the models may be trained on data containing human decisions or on data that reflect second-order effects of social or historical inequities.

This a crucial element for a bank Treasury, since it is the 'bank within the bank' and effectively functions as a clearing house for capital and funding, which is often driven by the underlying behaviour of customers. For example, one of the key Treasury activities is Funds Transfer Pricing (FTP), which assigns an internal price for funding sources like deposits and charges out the cost of funds to assets, like loans which require funding. FTP is rooted in the behavioural science of clients i.e. in terms of how long the funding remains with the bank (i.e. stability), or how quickly customers pay-back their loans. This behaviour is driven by many factors including: geographical location, income, access to different banking channels and others. Treasury therefore has to be aware of these elements and how they can influence its decision-making ability, when using more advanced digital technologies.

This awareness can be achieved by ensuring processes are in place to maximize fairness and minimize bias created by technologies like Artificial Intelligence (AI) e.g.

- Identify where there is a high risk that AI could exacerbate bias or help correct for the bias;
- Establish processes and practices to test for and mitigate bias in AI systems;
- Recognise that potential biases in human decisions exist and how this can flow into models; and
- Invest more in bias research and make more data available for research (while respecting privacy).

Fairness also relates to ethics. The development, deployment and use of any intelligent solution should adhere to some fundamental ethical principles such as respect for human autonomy, prevention of harm, explainability and guarantee that the outputs are free from unfair bias and prejudice, whether conscious or unconscious.

The risk for a Treasury is that if it does not address these considerations upfront, it could lead to Legal, Operational and Reputational issues down the line.

4.4 Risk Driver 4 - Data Protection and Quality

Data is a very valuable commodity and therefore it must be well protected. Data has always been the cornerstone of finance - from primitive ledgers to today's hyper-connected markets.

As mentioned, Treasury has a somewhat unique position in the bank since it holds a lot of data, ranging from customer level data to risk management data.

The first consideration for a Treasury is that it is critical that this information is well defended against internal and external threats. In a traditional set-up, it is normally protected by the banks centralised security measures, but this challenge can magnify significantly if data/information is moved to distributed cloud computing. This is one of the reasons why central banks historically were hesitant to fully endorse aspects like cloud-based computing [30]. However, this is not stopping new banks to venture down this route. Volt a new Australian online bank will only use cloud-based computing. While potential Volt customers are largely unaware of the distinction between public and private clouds, they are concerned about their data and how it is used. Volt is therefore developing a data policy for distributed data, that will be overseen by independent committees and that it hopes will be adopted by other Australian banks [20].

A second consideration is that when managing customer data, e.g. for behavioural profile of clients, a digital technology solution like Big Data and Advanced Analytics needs to comply to current regulation on data protection. This means the bank should have a lawful basis for processing the personal data. In addition, customers have the right to demand human intervention and not be subject to a decision based solely on automated process e.g. profiling, if the outcome impacts the customer in a significant manner [13].

Another issue for a Treasury is that the quality of data it uses might not always be that robust, since it can originate from fragmented bank systems which is not always aligned in terms of format or standards. Therefore, there is an obligation on Treasury to check the data quality and discard any low-quality inputs before it feeds into the digital models. An important point is that digital technology is not a panacea to fix bad quality data (meaning garbage in equals garbage out); using bad quality data to drive Big

Data and Machine Learning, can magnify the errors and lead to wrong decisions being made. Therefore, a Treasury needs to work very closely with upstream data providers to confirm the data quality, scrub the data and discard any data sources which do not meet its defined checks and balances.

4.5   Risk Driver 5 - International Standards

Treasury driven solutions are increasingly becoming more advanced and offering clients improved and real-time access to information and payments. As an example, HSBC has recently announced the launch of a Treasury Application Programming Interface (API) covering payments in 27 markets in a bid to offer business clients a faster and more seamless way to transfer funds [2]. Using HSBC Treasury APIs, Treasurers can make payments from their own workstations, without logging into a proprietary bank platform. Clients receive confirmation that a payment request has been received and can track payments from their accounts to the beneficiary, improving visibility over transactions.

APIs are facilitating a key shift towards more open banking by removing barriers between applications and systems and enabling seamless interaction between these different platforms. However, to ensure a level playing field for all competitors including well-regulated bank Treasuries and loosely controlled Fintech challengers, common standards are required. Data standards and protocols are the bedrock of a robust and dynamic financial system. They can enable innovation and competition and reduce the cost of finance. However, standards need to be consistent for all participants as it pertains to privacy, security, trust, resilience etc.

The risk for a Treasury is that in the absence of clearly defined standards around the deployment of digital technology, it either does nothing and thereby lose touch with wider market developments or proceed and implement solutions, which does not meet future requirements. Consistent data standards could bring several benefits to many different banking areas that Treasury interacts with:

- Innovations in retail payments, built-on common data standards and protocols, can enhance the understanding of client habits and transform deposit product developments;
- Access to wider data sets could allow more tailored and accurate decisions about lending, opening new borrowing opportunities for customers and small businesses;
- Big Data can help provide an in-depth understanding of business models for credit assessment; and
- Transferring data through APIs could give households and businesses better information about and access to financial products.

4.6   Risk Driver 6 - Business Continuation

A bank's Treasury normally has a number of activities that needs to be executed daily or even intraday, for example payment and settlements [11]. This real-time management and reporting requirement make it challenging for a Treasury to implement any new technology, given the potential impact on business continuation. A further difficulty for a typical Treasury function is that it operates in a technology environment that often comprises of largescale legacy systems, like cash management systems, which uses older technology which is not very adaptable for new requirements. Also, Treasury normally does not own the upstream data systems like product and pricing platforms, which makes it very difficult to implement any major changes. The reality is that Treasury is very intertwined with many different business divisions within the bank; therefore, making implementation of digital technology tricky, given the significant repercussions on business continuity if something goes wrong.

The one thing a bank cannot allow is to go offline, it is truly a 24/7 business, where even in the middle of night, batch operations run to process the previous day's transactions. Treasury digitalisation therefore, at least initially, needs to identify business cases to target which are more controllable or can be run separately as prototypes, before switching off life bank systems. Examples of these Treasury applications areas are:

- Big Data and Advanced Analytics used for financial planning and forecasting purposes,
- Machine Learning deployed to identify customer behaviour, and
- Robotic Process Automation implanted to automate certain Treasury owned processes.

As Treasury becomes more comfortable with digital technology deployment and proof its feasibility to senior management, it can be expanded to larger scale projects across the bank's wider technology infrastructure.

4.7 Risk Driver 7 - Technical Knowledge and Skills

The conundrum with digital technology implementation is that the required digital skills often resides in the technology department or some of the client-facing business areas and not in Treasury.

Treasury personnel's expertise often tend to be in disciplines such as capital management, liquidity management, portfolio management, which are specialised banking or finance skills. The business and technology skillsets in terms of training and education more often than not do not overlap. This is one of the key reasons, why digital technology adoption in Treasury is relatively low [1]. Treasury also do not have the same push-pressure to upskill, compared to other client interfacing business areas in the banks (e.g. mobile banking and fraud detection units).

Therefore, Treasury must emphasise upgrading its skills and employing new digital expertise instead of just focusing on traditional finance, tax and accountancy skillsets. If it does not expand its technical knowledge and expertise it will not be able to effectively reap the benefits of rolling out digital technology. Or it will implement digital solutions that it will struggle to maintain and manage going forward.

To be successful in an increasingly digitalised environment it must combine the right technology with the right talent. At a strategic level this will require that Treasury management build a digital vision and put together teams that are able to:

- understand the impact of digital technology on Treasury;
- articulate and champion the value of digital solutions to old Treasury problems;

- develop a strong business/technology foundation for digital transformation;
- partner and collaborate with other digital technology developments and teams in the bank; and
- implement and manage the required changes.

This section identified a range of risks and threats that a Treasury department should consider when implementing new digital technology. It is not an exhaustive list, but focused on the main challenges, which can impede the successful deployment of new digital technology. The next section will look at how these risks and threats can be managed in a holistic and integrated manner.

5   Managing Digital Risks and Threats in Treasury

It is important to manage the various risks and threats that can manifest from the adoption of new digital technology effectively. For a bank Treasury digitalisation often entails moving away from manually controlled processes, where the interpretation of results is based on personal experience and can be overridden if need be. Automation of processes and the introduction of intelligent algorithms can make many Treasury activities more effective, quicker and cost efficient, but it requires additional safeguards throughout the process to ensure the output is fair, explainable and unbiased. Also, leveraging technology like cloud computing have advantages, but it can move Treasury outside the security of its traditional defensive wall, which is often centralised and well protected behind the bank's wider computer security protocols.

There are various academic articles which looks at digital risk management in a digital economy such as [9] and within banks specifically [17, 21]. The section below tailors and refines these different risk management frameworks and approaches for a Treasury department. Figure 3 depicts the primary steps that can underpin a Treasury's digital risk management approach.

The next section looks at a risk management cycle that can be used in Treasury to manage the threats and risks in a more integrated manner.

5.1   Step 1 - Develop a Board Approved Risk Appetite Policy

As identified in the AFP survey [1] many banks do not have a board approved policy for digital risks. In cases where a digital policy does exist, it is often focussed on the client interfacing business activities, and not specifically on functions like Treasury.

As mentioned, Treasury has an important role and responsibility within the bank because it interacts with a lot of external counterparts and internal businesses and are involved with various transactional systems.

It is therefore crucial that the Treasurer works with the Board and the Risk Management division to ensure that a digital risk policy is formulated and that it includes Treasury activities [30]. This is required to define a formal digital risk appetite for the firm and provide guidance to Treasury on what digital technologies it can focus on. It will also ensure that the right governance and oversight is in place for any future implementation.

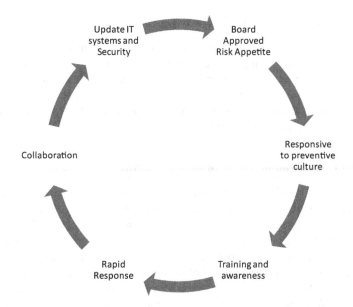

Fig. 3. Managing digital risks and threats in Treasury arising from digital technology adoption

5.2   Step 2 - Evolve from a Defensive to an Offensive Environment

Digital technologies often expand the footprint of the bank. This opens up a lot more avenues of attack that can be used to hack into the bank's or Treasury's systems to steal valuable data and/or smart models. This digital expansion requires that security measures must evolve from being primarily defensive to becoming more offensive in nature. This means that policy, systems and the culture need to be reengineered, not just to protect the bank's 'valuable assets' against cyber-attacks, but also to pre-emptively identify and eliminate threats before it occurs.

5.3   Step 3 - Training and Awareness on Digital Technology Risks

As mentioned previously it is crucial that training and awareness of digital technology risks takes place in Treasury. The reasons are two-fold:

1. Digital technology utilisation can often create new risks and threats that has limited reference points with traditional banking activity. For example, cyber theft of money or data sounds straight-forward, but the ways and means hackers can attack the bank can vary significantly (in contrast to an old-style bank robbery). Furthermore, the use of intelligent models for decision-making purposes can create outcomes, which is not anticipated.
2. Normally personnel in areas like Treasury and Finance do not have a technology background. It is therefore crucial that they are educated on the use and risks of digital technology and that teams are expanded to include individuals with technology experience.

5.4   Step 4 - Real-Time Threat Monitoring

Digital technology offers many benefits, one being that it can improve the frequency of certain Treasury activities to almost real-time e.g. intra-day liquidity management [11], or client API payment execution [2]. This means protective measures need to evolve to become more rapid responsive. If something goes wrong or a threat materialise it needs to be identified and addressed immediately. This is a paradigm shift for many Treasuries that are used to operating on a slower timescale.

5.5   Step 5 - Collaboration and Information Sharing

The real success of digital technology implementation and combatting digital threats reside in taking a unified approach across the firm. Many banks are relatively digital mature as it pertains to client facing applications like online banking and fraud detection and therefore have the relevant digital skills and experience in place. However, digital maturity is not always uniform across the organisation. As indicated, Treasuries tends to be slow adopters of digital technology. Rather than re-invent the wheel and starting from scratch, it can really benefit from collaborating with other business units and through the sharing of information. This will ensure the bank's digital strategy is integrated and consistently implemented.

5.6   Step 6 - Update/Revise IT Systems and Security

Implementing any new technology including digital technology may require an update to existing IT systems and security measures. These can include inter-alia: preform a security audit to reveal the strengths and weaknesses of the existing setup, strengthen the existing firewalls, update anti-virus and anti-malware applications and consider enhanced authentication like biometrics, too obtain access confidential data and/or models.

6   Further Development and Research

This paper studied the risk and threats that can arise from the adoption of Digital Technology in Treasury. Identifying and protecting against digital risks cannot happen in isolation, but needs to form part of a unified digital transformation plan that inter-alia includes elements such as business case development, selecting appropriate digital technology and its implementation, as well as protective measures against new digital threats.

Therefore, the management of digital risks and threats described in this paper forms an integral part of the overarching Smart Digital Treasury Model (SDTM). The intention is that once completed the SDTM will be tested with a number of bank Treasuries to validate the feasibility and robustness of the model. This user acceptance phase will include evaluation of the risk management building block as well. Based on the market practitioner feedback it will either move forward for adoption or if required further research and modification will be undertaken.

7 Conclusion

The role and responsibility of a Treasury department within a commercial bank has changed significantly over the last couple of decades and especially since the financial crisis. During this time, a bank's Treasury function has evolved from being primarily focussed on activities like cash management to becoming the guardian of the holistic balance sheet.

Comprehensive digitalisation of Treasury can help support this expanding mandate and can deliver a range of commercial benefits, for example reduce operating costs and enhance Net Interest Income. The problem is that Treasury tends to be a slow adopter of digital technology and often does not have a well-articulated digital strategy. The Smart Digital Treasury Model (SDTM) was developed with the objective to provide a bank Treasury a well-defined roadmap to transition towards becoming a more mature digital user.

As part of digital transition, it is important to identify and manage any risks and threats that may arise due to the adoption of new digital technology. For a bank Treasury it often entails transitioning away from manually controlled processes, where the interpretation of results is based on experience and can be overridden. Automation of processes and the introduction of intelligent algorithms can make many Treasury activities, more effective, quicker and cost efficient, but it requires safeguards throughout the process to ensure the output is fair, explainable and safe. Also, leveraging technology like cloud computing have a range of benefits, but it moves Treasury outside its traditional security defence, which is often centralised and well protected behind the bank's wider computer security protocols.

The contribution of this paper is in researching an approach that identifies the main threats and risks that a Treasury should take cognisance off, when adopting new digital technology. It also describes a risk management framework to assess and manage these digital risks in a holistic manner across Treasury. The digital landscape is evolving the whole time; therefore, this digital risk management process can't be managed in isolation or seen as a once-off exercise, but needs to be part of an integrated digital transformation plan.

References

1. AFP. AFP Risk Survey Report. Treasury Risk Survey Report. Association of Finance Professional (2018). https://www.oliverwyman.com/our-expertise/insights/2018/jan/2018-afp-risk-survey-report.html
2. Ashar, J.: HSBC Launches Treasury APIs for Payments in 27 Markets (2020). https://www.theglobaltreasurer.com/2020/01/15/hsbc-launches-treasury-apis-for-payments-in-27-markets/
3. Association of Finance Professionals: AFP Strategic Role of Treasury Survey. Association of Finance Professional Library (2017)
4. Barrigar, Z.: Examining the Current Threat of Cybercrime in Mobile Banking and What Can Be Done to Combat It - ProQuest. Utica College: ProQuest Dissertations Publishing (2020)
5. Bauer, Stefan, Bernroider, Edward W.N.: From information security awareness to reasoned compliant action: analysing information security policy compliance in a large banking organization. ACM SIGMIS Database DATABASE Adv. Inf. Syst. **48**(3), 44–68 (2017). https://doi.org/10.1145/3130515.3130519

6. Bragg, S.: Treasury Management: The Practitioner's Guide. Hoboken, N.J. (2010)
7. Camillo, Mark: Cybersecurity: risks and management of risks for global banks and financial institutions. J. Risk Manage. Financ. Inst. **10**(2), 196–200 (2017)
8. Ceren, J., Montegelli, S.: Trends in technology: how web 2.0 will impact the next generation of online treasury tools. J. Corp. Treasury Manage. **1**(1), 78–82, 5 (2007)
9. Chernyakov, M., Chernyakova, M.: Technological risks of the digital economy. Корпоративные Финансы **12**(4) (2018). https://cyberleninka.ru/article/n/technological-risks-of-the-digital-economy
10. Daniel, W.K., William, K.F., Ling, M.L., Lai, S.M., Tevanotai, A.: Awareness in E-banking security and usage. In: 2014 International Conference on Information Science, Electronics and Electrical Engineering, vol. 2, pp. 1176–1150 (2014). https://doi.org/10.1109/InfoSEEE.2014.6947856
11. Davies, A., Wheaton, M., Stambaugh, T., Wilson, M.: Intraday Liquidity Management|Accenture. Accenture Consulting (2019). https://www.accenture.com/gb-en/insights/financial-services/intraday-liquidity-management
12. Di Paola, S., Cohen, E., Farrar, I.: Global Treasury Benchmarking Survey 2019. PwC 2019 (2019). https://www.pwc.com/gx/en/services/audit-assurance/publications/global-treasury-benchmarking-survey-2019.html
13. EBA. EBA Report Identifies Key Challenges in the Roll out of Big Data and Advanced Analytics. European Banking Authority, 13 January 2020. https://eba.europa.eu/eba-report-identifies-key-challenges-roll-out-big-data-and-advanced-analytics
14. Elgeti, C., Schäfer, R., Vogt, P., Broemstrup, I., Lai, C., Granzer, M., Strauch, T.: Creating a Digital Treasury in Banking. Boston Consulting Group (2019)
15. FSA: Senior Asset and Liability Management Committee Practices. Financial Services Authority Library (2010)
16. Harrison, T., Estelami, H.: The Routledge Companion to Financial Services Marketing. Routledge Publishing, London (2014)
17. Harvey, David: Digital transformation in banks: the trials, opportunities and a guide to what is important. J. Digital Bank. **1**(2), 136–145 (2016)
18. HKMA. High-Level Principles on Artificial Intelligence. Hong Kong Monetary Authority (2019)
19. Mbelli, T.M., Dwolatzky, B.: Cyber security, a threat to cyber banking in South Africa: an approach to network and application security. In: 2016 IEEE 3rd International Conference on Cyber Security and Cloud Computing (CSCloud), pp. 1–6 (2016). https://doi.org/10.1109/CSCloud.2016.18
20. Mistry, D.: Banks with Their Feet on the Ground Should Have Their Heads in the Cloud. International Banker (2019). https://internationalbanker.com/technology/banks-with-their-feet-on-the-ground-should-have-their-heads-in-the-cloud/
21. Moloi, Tankiso, Iredele, Oluwamayowa Olalekan: Risk management in the digital era: the case of nigerian banks. In: George, Babu, Paul, Justin (eds.) Digital Transformation in Business and Society, pp. 229–246. Springer, Cham (2020). https://doi.org/10.1007/978-3-030-08277-2_14
22. Pattinson, Malcolm., Butavicius, Marcus., Parsons, Kathryn., McCormac, Agata, Calic, Dragana: Managing information security awareness at an australian bank: a comparative study. Inf. Comput. Secur. **25**(2), 181–189 (2017). https://doi.org/10.1108/ICS-03-2017-0017
23. Phillips, Aaron L.: Treasury management: job responsibilities, curricular development, and research opportunities. Financ. Manage. **26**(3), 69–81 (1997). https://doi.org/10.1111/%28ISSN%291755-053X/issues
24. Polak, P.: Centralization of Treasury Management in a Globalized World. SSRN Scholarly Paper ID 1702687. Rochester, NY: Social Science Research Network (2010). https://papers.ssrn.com/abstract=1702687

25. Ramskogler, Paul: Tracing the origins of the financial crisis. OECD J. Finan. Market Trends **2014**(2), 47–61 (2015). https://doi.org/10.1787/fmt-2014-5js3dqmsl4br
26. Sarkanova, B.: The Impact of Selected Financial Regulations on Corporate Treasury Management. vol. IV. QUAERE 2016 (2016)
27. Schmitz, S.W., Wood, G.: Institutional Change in the Payments System and Monetary Policy. Routledge (2007)
28. Sironi, A.: The evolution of banking regulation since the financial crisis: a critical assessment. SSRN Scholarly Paper ID 3304672. Rochester, NY: Social Science Research Network (2018). https://doi.org/10.2139/ssrn.3304672
29. Tounsi, W., Rais, H.: A survey on technical threat intelligence in the age of sophisticated cyber attacks. Comput. Secur. **72**, 212–233 (2018). https://doi.org/10.1016/j.cose.2017.09.001
30. Van Steenis, H.: Future of Finance: Review on the Outlook for the UK Financial System (2019). https://www.bankofengland.co.uk/-/media/boe/files/report/2019/future-of-finance-report.pdf?la=en&hash=59CEFAEF01C71AA551E7182262E933A699E952FC
31. Von Solms, J.: (Forthcoming) Digital Technology Adoption in a Bank Treasury and Performing a Digital Maturity Assessment (2020)
32. Von Solms, J., Langerman, J.: A Smart Treasury Fit for the 4th Industrial Revolution. FEMIB 2020 (2020). https://www.insticc.org/node/TechnicalProgram/femib/2020/personDetails/00e65df0-5615-4a51-809b-60a49ef97d3f

Cyber Security Canvas for SMEs

Stephanie Teufel$^{(\boxtimes)}$, Bernd Teufel, Mohammad Aldabbas, and Minh Nguyen

International Institute of Management in Technology (Iimt), University of Fribourg, 1700 Fribourg, Switzerland
stephanie.teufel@unifr.ch

Abstract. In an increasingly digitalized and networked world, information security and cyber security pose ever greater challenges to organizations. Cyber-attacks cause high economic damage and can bring organizations to ruin. Many small and medium-sized enterprises (SME) are under the illusion that only the large companies are the victims of an attack; they protect their valuable data against this background only poorly. But even in research, the focus is generally not on SMEs. In the context of this work, an easy-to-use Cyber Security Canvas is therefore being modelled to close this gap and to allow SMEs pragmatic access to the topic. The model framework is supplemented with modular building blocks. The building blocks can be put together individually according to the requirements and needs of the SMEs using them, with the model dividing them up according to priority. The newly designed Cyber Security Canvas was put through an application test with a European-based SME in order to gain first insights into its practical suitability in the European context. The model proved to be successful, and was well received by the participant. Nevertheless, it has potential for improvement.

Keywords: Cyber security canvas · Security framework · SME

1 Security Research and SMEs

The global, digital interconnection of the professional world increases the need for security in all areas. Not only does it offer potential for prosperity, it also opens up new areas of attack on companies, and increasingly on SMEs (small and medium-sized enterprises) as well. To ensure secure systems, all computer users should safely interact with these systems [1]. According to a survey on behalf of the Austrian techbold technology Group AG [2] in January 2020, one third of all companies with up to 30 employees in Austria have had an IT security incident in the last two years; in companies with more than 30 employees, 60% were already affected. For SMEs, existential threats are increasingly shifting from the analog world to the digital world. The areas of threat are constantly changing and expanding, while the majority of resources and financial means of defense are stagnating, especially for SMEs. Simple and yet targeted support measures are therefore required.

Hardly a day goes by without media reports of data thefts or paralyzed organizations due to professional cyber-attacks. Such disruptions cause great economic damage and can bankrupt an organization. Many SMEs are under the misconception that only the large

© Springer Nature Switzerland AG 2020
H. Venter et al. (Eds.): ISSA 2020, CCIS 1339, pp. 20–33, 2020.
https://doi.org/10.1007/978-3-030-66039-0_2

corporations are victims of an attack and do not protect their valuable data sufficiently against this background. SMEs tend to ignore the importance of applying effective information security measures which leaves them vulnerable to big losses [3]. Berry et al. [4] also notes that larger companies have resources to deal with cyber security issues, while small companies often do not have the resources to do so.

Parts of the inherent reasons behind these reported disruptions are purely human factors, where the users of the digitalized applications make naive mistakes that lead to a breach in the system, making it vulnerable and prone to outsiders [5]. Wiercioch et al. [6] argue that users value convenience or quick access over security. This is a phenomenon that is particularly common among smaller SMEs. The human being, i.e. the person responsible for an SME whether the owner or the manager, remains a major risk factor due to his or her behavior, action or inaction; he or she is the weakest point in terms of security. [7–9]. However, gaps are also apparent in research in this respect. Hence, Ref. [10] shows that "organizational IT security research has largely neglected the SME context." The results of the research of [10] imply that common assumptions such as the availability of a qualified workforce, documented processes or IT budget planning have to be modified in the security discussion for SMEs.

In order to close this gap, an easy-to-use Cyber Security Canvas is modelled in this paper. The model framework follows the "one-size-fits-all" principle and is completed with modular building blocks. The building blocks can be individually assembled according to the requirements and needs of the applying organization, with the model subdividing them according to urgency. The Cyber Security Canvas is based on already existing frameworks such as ISO/IEC 27001, the IT-Grundschutz of the German Federal Office for Information Security and the NIST framework from the US.

The Cyber Security Canvas developed is intended to enable SMEs that do not have their own IT specialists and a correspondingly large IT budget to meet at least the basic requirements for corporate cyber security and to raise awareness of the issue. The canvas was subjected to an initial test in the form of an interview with an SME regarding its comprehensibility and applicability. Hence, the type of errors that this canvas is intended to avoid are the unintentional human errors in using technology, not the provision of technological solutions. For further reading on human errors in utilization of technology, see [5].

The authors would like to emphasize at this point that they are well aware of the different views on the terms "information security" and "cyber security". According to Ref. [11] "cyber security needs to be seen as an expansion of information security". Correspondingly, not an information security canvas but a cyber security canvas is modelled.

2   A Brief Overview of Information Security Management Systems and Security Frameworks

Anything used to monitor the essential objectives and their maintenance is called a management system (MS) [12]. By means of such MSs it can be quickly determined which information security risks are highly relevant and which can be maintained. From the company's point of view, such a system combines efficiency and effectiveness at the same time [13]. One of the most important reasons for the development and introduction of an MS is to move away from an ad hoc organization and thus to define and describe workflows, procedures or processes in general. Certainly, this approach is essential for the area of information security as well.

Böhmer et al. [13] define an Information Security Management System (ISMS) as follows: "An ISMS is a systematic model for the introduction, implementation, operation, monitoring, review, maintenance and improvement of the organization's information security to achieve business objectives. It is based on a risk assessment and the risk acceptance level of the organization and is designed to effectively manage the risks. An analysis of the requirements for the protection of information assets and the application of appropriate measures to ensure the protection of these information assets as required contributes to the successful implementation of an ISMS."

It should be noted that an ISMS is generally only one part of a more general, comprehensive management system. So, if a company already has management tools or similar systems, e.g. another ISO certification, it should be checked whether parts of them can also be used for a planned ISMS in order to optimize the implementation and operation of the ISMS.

2.1 Structure and Functions of an ISMS

Typically, the structure of a MS consists of the following (sub-)tasks [12]:

- Goals are formulated in the form of guidelines.
- Risks and opportunities are analysed for the formulated goals.
- Roles and responsibilities for the achievement of the goals or sub-goals are defined.
- Persons affected by the issue must give up their specific regulations or guidelines.
- Processes and procedures are redefined and implemented (including the necessary measures).
- The achievement of objectives must be evaluated, which is why the processes required for this must be planned.

By defining the structure, it quickly becomes clear that roles such as the IT security officer or the organizational unit IT security management are only parts of an ISMS. The misunderstanding regarding the role and function occurs frequently, because the scope of an ISMS usually affects the whole company.

The focus of an ISMS lies in the maintenance of information security and fulfils the tasks of defining goals, implementing measures, integrating into work and operational processes, monitoring and checking. An ISMS is a continuous improvement process which is best described by a PDCA cycle (Plan-Do-Check-Act, also known as the Shewhart-Deming PDCA cycle) [14], which is why maintenance and further development are equally important tasks [8].

2.2 ISO/IEC 27001

ISO/IEC 27001 is the internationally recognized standard for ISMS and provides specifications and requirements for an ISMS [15]. It should be noted that the standard itself recognises that an ISMS "shall be scaled according to the requirements of the organisation" and it is assumed that the ISMS "will change over time". Any organization that operates an ISMS and wishes to certify to the ISO/IEC 27001 standard must follow the specifications contained in the standard.

The analysis of the ISO/IEC 27001 standard is important for the development of a Cyber Security Canvas because the standard is scalable, organization-independent and enjoys worldwide acceptance. The standard defines the requirements for the introduction, implementation, operation, monitoring, review, maintenance and improvement of an ISMS, which can be tailored to the organization [13].

2.3 BSI IT-Grundschutz Catalogues

The IT-Grundschutz of the German Federal Office for Information Security (BSI) was developed to increase information security in organizations of all types and sizes. The BSI catalogues IT-Grundschutz are regarded as a benchmark for the development of an ISMS. The BSI standards are the foundation for information security and contain methods and procedures for various topics in the field of information security [16].

The effort and costs for certification according to ISO 27001 on the basis of IT Grundschutz are significantly higher than for certification according to ISO 27001 alone [17]. The BSI standard enjoys an excellent reputation with regard to its benefits, primarily in Germany due to its origin, and is also cited in European guidelines as a reference model, but has limited acceptance internationally.

2.4 NIST-Framework

The NIST framework was first published by the US National Institute of Standards and Technology (NIST) in 2014 and revised in 2017 and 2018. Originally, the framework was developed with a focus on the critical infrastructures of public authorities, but it also explicitly addresses companies in the public or private sector [18]. For the authorities in the US, these standards are mandatory [16]. Regardless of the size of the company or the extent of the effective cyber security risks, the NIST framework provides guidance and best practices to improve the security structure and resilience of companies with respect to cyber security [18]. However, the framework is not a universal tool for cyber security prevention and defence, but must be adapted to the individual threat situation of a company.

Either the NIST framework can be seen as a supplement to the already existing cyber security measures of a company or as a completely new basis for the introduction of appropriate measures. This framework shows the current security status and the limits of an organisation, but can offer very good suggestions for action and measures, especially in the area of critical infrastructures [18].

Information Security Management Systems and Security Frameworks, as described above, provide the basis for designing a Cyber Security Canvas, as shown in the following section. Special attention was paid to the fact that the specific complexity of these frameworks can be translated into a practical, easy-to-use setting.

2.5   Bottom Line for Canvas Design

For the design of a Cyber Security Canvas the presented frameworks offer a lot of inspiration, which has to be individualized in the corresponding context. NIST tend to be security control oriented which contains a vast possibility of groups to enable best practices linked to federal information systems. ISO focuses on less technicality and more on risk as focal point. ISO is applicable for organizations of different sizes and shapes. BSI is applied usually to provide technical support for users of information technology [16]. Due to the qualities of ISO and NEST, and for the purpose of this paper, these two will be used in designing the core of the Canvas.

3   Shaping a Cyber Security Canvas

In Ref. [17], ISMS and the security frameworks briefly described in the previous section were analysed and evaluated, and it was shown how the insights gained can be incorporated into the modelling of a Cyber Security Canvas. The Cyber Security Canvas is mainly based on their theoretical foundation.

3.1   Design of the Prototype

At the beginning of the study, after a rough review of suitable technical literature, a prototype was created with various possible influencing factors. Figure 1 (prototype of the model) represents a rough structuring of potential influencing factors, whose relevance for the Cyber Security Canvas is to be examined with the help of suitable technical literature and already existing models and frameworks. In a second step, the influencing factors are analysed in the main theory parts and, if they are suitable in the sense of being applicable, cost efficient and yield results, are transferred to the further conception, otherwise they are discarded.

Further influencing factors from the preceding topics such as ISMS, ISO 27001 and the NIST framework are continuously added and explained during the modelling process, since the basis of the Cyber Security Canvas is mainly based on their theoretical foundation.

3.2   Advanced Design Abstraction of the Prototype

After analyzing the technical literature, it can be concluded that the inclusion of case studies from IT security is rather unimportant for the development of the Cyber Security Canvas. This is due to the overriding importance of the models examined in relation to the topics of information security and cyber security. Practical case studies enjoy only a subordinate relevance, since models such as ISO 27001 or NIST Framework focus on the theoretical model framework. These institutions continuously publish recommendations for action and guidelines, and often specialized institutes from the private sector take care of implementation and certification.

The remaining six factors from Fig. 1 are relevant for the Cyber Security Canvas (for details see [17]) and will be directly incorporated into the final model.

Fig. 1. First prototype and possible influencing factors.

3.3 Cyber Security Canvas

Figure 2 shows the end of the modeling phase with the final framework.

The Cyber Security Canvas is a top-down strategy, which implies that the change process must be initiated by the top management. The strategy and approach with regard to the overall goals of the company (in this case the information security or cyber security strategy) is defined by top management and from there, as a derivation of strategic goals, reaches the organization (operational level) downwards. The advantage of the top-down strategy is the role model function and credibility, which is exemplified by top management [19]. Employees are thus more motivated and the strategic goals communicated at the operational level enjoy the necessary support, which promotes the sustainable development of the organization [20].

The blue frame around the model indicates the (digital) corporate environment and the stakeholders who have a legitimate interest in the company. These can be, for example, customers, suppliers or competitors. A process-oriented 5-layer model (layers 1–5) is derived from a simplification and through complexity reduction from the models ISO 27001, IT-Grundschutz of the BSI and the NIST framework, whereby the layers have a mutual interaction and are by no means static.

Further characteristics of this model are the individuality as well as the possible modular structure with five modules per layer, which can be individually combined according to the requirements and specifications of the company. This enables the applicability to all organizations and sectors, as the needs of a public authority are very different from those of a small business. At the beginning of the study, this was one of the central points or conditions to be fulfilled by the model, along with scalability.

(Digital) Corporate Environment and Stakeholders

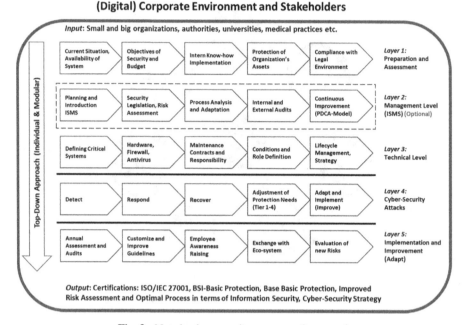

Fig. 2. Novel cyber security canvas as framework

3.4 Structure and Scalability of the Model

The Cyber Security Canvas combines all relevant components from the three models examined and presents them graphically as a top-down approach. The layered and modular structure clearly presents all the issues facing the organization. As a guideline, it can be explained that the user basically moves from top to bottom (layer 1 to layer 5 according to the top-down approach), but is not restricted in his flexibility. If no ISMS is to be introduced, layer 2 can simply be skipped. The modular structure in the form of process modules has the advantage that the sequence of implementation only has to be adhered to in some process chains such as Detect-Respond-Recover, but otherwise the user is quite free in his selection/implementation. Building blocks that are not required for the achievement of the organization's objectives can be skipped just like the layers. Whether all steps must be carried out also depends to a large extent on the expected output. If an organization decides to be certified according to ISO 27001, it will be forced to work through all steps and building blocks (especially with regard to the introduction of an ISMS).

Figure 3 shows that the scalability and applicability of the model is given for all organizations, authorities and associations of all sectors due to its modular structure.

Layer 1: Preparation and assessment.

This layer is initiated and accompanied by the management or by the managing director. In contrast to other models, where an ISMS is introduced at the very beginning, this level is only concerned with preparation and internal assessment. Ideally, the organization starts with a combination of the first two building blocks and reflects the actual

(Digital) Corporate Environment and Stakeholders

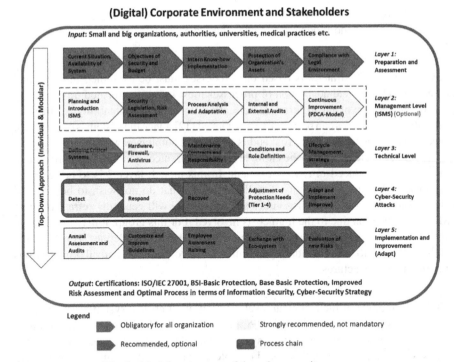

Fig. 3. Modular structure of the cyber security canvas.

situation. This also takes one of the four dimensions of IT security into account, namely availability. This value is either already available as a key figure or the measurement of availability is planned and introduced for the first time with this step. The starting point of the entire framework is the derivation of security objectives of the company, not only with regard to information security and cyber security strategy, but also with regard to individual orientation and available resources (budget).

The third step is to analyze whether the know-how for the implementation of the required objectives is available internally or whether additional specialists need to be sought externally. The sub-goals have to be distributed specifically to different employees so that everyone knows their role and responsibilities. If, depending on the country, the organization belongs to the category "critical infrastructure", which may also apply to SMEs, all four dimensions of IT security must even be fulfilled. In Germany, for example, their fulfilment must be continuously demonstrated to the BSI. This goes hand in hand with the final building block of the "Legal Environment and Compliance" model, since companies in certain sectors (energy, information technology, telecommunications, transport and traffic, health, water, food, and finance and insurance) are obliged to take appropriate technical precautions to protect their infrastructure and must, for example, be certified according to an ISO system. With an ISO certificate, the guarantee of information security is demonstrated to the corporate environment and stakeholders.

Layer 2: Management Level (ISMS).

According to all the models presented, this level explains the introduction of an ISMS.

An important factor for Layer 2 is the creation of an organization-wide security policy, which the IT strategy is based on. Processes must be examined in detail and adapted. The change and adaptation of processes must be communicated transparently to the employees involved in terms of role allocation and accountability, so that the organization's objectives can be effectively achieved [12]. Once the system is established, it must undergo internal and external audits to ensure compliance with the guidelines.

The PDCA cycle applies to the entire level and guarantees continuous improvement of the system introduced in risk assessment. In this model, layer 2 is to be regarded as optional rather than mandatory. Small companies that do not wish to be certified or do not have the appropriate resources and know-how will generally refrain from an ISMS or certification due to the high costs involved. For this group, it may make sense to move towards the basic assurance as described in the BSI guidelines. However, the introduction of an ISMS is mandatory for authorities, corporations and all organizations with critical infrastructures.

Layer 3: Technical level.

The first module of the technical level "Definition of critical systems" is similar to the module "Assets of the organization/Protect" on layer 1, but it refers to the physical IT systems of an organization. Critical systems can be, for example, productive servers, databases or backup systems that could completely paralyze the company in the event of an attack. Further implementation measures also include the evaluation or acquisition of suitable components such as a firewall or endpoint protection (antivirus software).

If the corresponding know-how is not available internally, maintenance contracts should be concluded with specialized IT suppliers so that continuous maintenance and thus the level of protection is contractually guaranteed. This allows certain responsibilities and risks to be outsourced to the IT supplier at the same time. In the interests of long-term and sustainable lifecycle management, a concept for the regular replacement of critical systems and hardware can be developed in collaboration with various IT suppliers. Lifecycle management should fit in with the organization-wide IT strategy in line with the security policy, so that proactive rather than reactive action is taken when necessary. This helps to keep the availability of the systems according to layer 1 high.

Layer 4: Cyber security attacks.

Cyber security prevention in this model is strongly based on the NIST framework. The first three building blocks "Detect, Respond and Recover" are identical to the structure of the NIST Framework Core, whereby all activities and layers in this model should support cyber security prevention and avoid attacks at all. However, if a system has already been attacked, it must first be detected (Detect) in order for an appropriate response to occur (Respond), and then the system must be restored to a functional state (Recover) [18]. For further details see [17].

As soon as the systems are operational again, an in-depth analysis of the attack or data loss should be made so that conclusions can be drawn about the need for protection and the organization can prepare for future attacks [18]. Thus, the context of the four NIST Implementation Tiers is restored here.

Layer 5: Implementation and improvement (Adapt).

The ultimate layer of the model relates to the continuous development and adaptation of the security policy, processes, and awareness. Employees are one of the key success factors, provided they see a benefit in the adaptations and changes. The organization should therefore spend resources and time on training employees and increasing their cyber security awareness [12].

A continuous exchange of information with the corporate environment and stakeholders brings new insights into the areas of information security and cyber security, which in turn can improve risk management.

As soon as an organization has implemented and completed at least layers 1 and 2, it can be certified at the end, as an output of the model, according to ISO 27001 or according to the basic IT protection of the BSI. With the implementation of the modules from layer 4, it fulfils a large part of the requirements of the NIST framework without having to be certified (in the sense of a self-assessment). The three terms "Detect", "Respond" and "Recover" were shaded blue in Fig. 3, as they exactly reflect the elements and procedures of the NIST framework. It can therefore be said that this model can be used to improve risk assessment (layer 1). Processes related to information security or cyber security prevention are no longer rigid, but are constantly being adapted to new circumstances.

All red fields from Fig. 3 are mandatory. It does not matter whether the organization is small or large. These are the basic requirements, which are strictly specified for a successful application of the model. The yellow fields are tasks the processing of which is highly recommended but not mandatory. The processing of the yellow fields strongly depends on the know-how, the skills and the motivation of the organization (also with regard to whether certification is sought or not). The green fields are also recommended in the application, but are to be considered as a subordinate supporting function and therefore voluntary. The mechanism of scalability is thus defined here by strict adherence to the various levels and process components.

This framework focuses on simplicity of use and a structured and simplified graphical representation. It attempts to reduce the complexity of the page-long sets of rules of the various frameworks presented and thus provides the user with a quick overview of the structure of the measures to be implemented without being too trivial in its approach.

3.5 Limits of the Model

This model has characteristics of a "one-size-fits-all" concept. This description applies in principle to the model frame, but the process modules can be combined variably and thus the model is extended by dynamic components. The model also takes into account the interactions with the (digital) corporate environment and stakeholders. Through this interaction, the model continuously adapts to the latest risks and hazards, which gives it a certain dynamism.

However, the limitations of the model will quickly become apparent if the details of the certification process become more detailed. As a first overview and assessment, the model is very helpful.

The elements used in the Canvas are mainly driven from the mentioned and discussed frameworks, then selected heuristically to be implemented. Therefore, the authors state that there is a margin for future improvement of the Canvas.

The goal of this development of a Cyber Security Canvas was to improve risk assessment, ease of use and economic benefit. Risk assessment and ease of use can be confirmed. The economic benefit is naturally difficult to prove. The costs of certification (internal and external) are also incurred when using the Cyber Security Canvas. The effective economic benefit is therefore the same as with the other models, provided that the certification is confirmed. If one had to measure the economic benefit, this would be, for example, the value of the cyber-attacks that might have been prevented (quantified as financial damage) or a possible loss of image due to the loss of customer data (quantified as "damage to reputation" with financial consequences due to a decline in sales). For a SME without a certification target, an economic benefit would be easier to measure, as the model, through its simple approach, increases awareness and motivation to implement technical and non-technical measures, thus forming an initial protection perimeter.

4   First Experience and Implications

The developed Cyber Security Canvas has been subjected to an application test at an SME to gain first insights into its practical suitability.

4.1   Baseline Situation and Test Design

The test design was originally planned as a before-and-after study with different test questions at two different points in time (longitudinal study), whereby the sample of two persons (N = 2, N represents the total population) would not have been representative. A quantitative analysis is therefore not possible, as the test quality criteria would have been difficult to meet under the given conditions. Quality criteria are an instrument for assessing the quality of scientific tests [21].

As an alternative, a qualitative survey with exploratory character was chosen. The test should examine the Cyber Security Canvas with regard to the following factors:

- Comprehensibility in terms of general applicability and graphic representation
- Comprehensibility and benefits of the individual process modules
- Benefit of the model in relation to the own needs

The duration of the interview was approximately 45–60 min, whereby a whole day was planned for the whole test including preparation and follow-up. The preparation time included in particular the coordination with the SME and the structure of the interview questions. No recommended actions were given, since the SME should not assess and evaluate itself, but primarily the model. In the last step, the collected answers were analyzed and evaluated.

4.2   Findings

The participant applied the framework at his business (in the pharmaceutical sector) and informed that the canvas proved to be easy to read and understand in practice. Due to the complexity of the subject area, it is easy to understand that further explanations in the form of an appendix could be added to the model to increase the usefulness and advantages of the model for the potential user.

The process orientation was mapped with the modules, although in practice it is rather difficult to put them into a context in purely conceptual terms. The interview conducted confirms this hypothesis, because the interviewee considers his general IT knowledge to be good, but could not always follow the explanations of the modules with his knowledge. Completion of the Cyber Security Canvas with a catalogue of measures would be desirable. On the one hand this can be seen as a weakness of the model and on the other hand as new knowledge that was only discovered with the development and modelling of the model.

4.3 Implications

An organization can use this model in the context of an initial self-assessment in order to rethink its processes and cyber security strategy as an initial introduction. In its novel structure, the holistic approach also includes the technical aspects that contribute to the fulfilment of cyber security prevention.

A Cyber Security Canvas is needed to get a quick first overview of the measures to be implemented. The overview summarizes important components from the examined frameworks, whereby the user benefits to a certain extent from a reduction in complexity, since he does not have to struggle individually through the various sets of rules and their appendices. As a first point of contact, the model helps to develop ideas for a possible approach, whereby the model attempts to cover all relevant dimensions and areas. The structure of the model is modular and can be adapted to the individual needs and objectives of the organization. A certain degree of flexibility is thus enabled, whereby the framework of the model must guide and support the user in its implementation. On the one hand, this is achieved by the top-down organization, on the other hand, different layers are mapped, which should serve the user as an orientation guide. The model can therefore be used as a basis for further development. The possibilities for development range from the elaboration of a concrete catalogue of measures (for example based on already existing frameworks) to graphic refinement and supplementation with further influencing factors, which are inexhaustible in the field of IT security. This approach is also recommended as an outlook, since information security and cyber security are constantly in a race against time. In our increasingly digitalized and networked world, maintaining data protection and preventing attacks is becoming an ever-greater challenge.

Acknowledgment. This work was supported by the Canton of Fribourg, Switzerland, through the Smart Living Lab project at the University of Fribourg.

References

1. Simonet, J., Teufel, S.: The Influence of Organizational, Social and Personal Factors on Cybersecurity Awareness and Behavior of Home Computer Users. In: Dhillon, G., Karlsson, F., Hedström, K., Zúquete, A. (eds.) ICT Systems Security and Privacy Protection. SEC 2019. IFIP Advances in Information and Communication Technology, vol 562. Springer, Cham (2019)
2. techbold technology Group AG: Studie Status IT-Sicherheit KMU Österreich 2020. Report. techbold technology group AG und MindTake Research GmbH, Wien (2020)
3. Bougaardt, G., Kyobe, M.: Investigating the factors inhibiting SMEs from recognizing and measuring losses from cybercrime in South Africa. In: ICIME 2011-Proceedings of the 2nd International Conference on Information Management and Evaluation, Toronto, Canada, pp. 62–70 (2011)
4. Berry, C., Berry, R.: An initial assessment of small business risk management approaches for cyber security threats. Int. J. Bus. Continuity Risk Manage. 8(1), 1–10 (2018)
5. Aldabbas, M., Teufel, B.: Human aspects of smart technologies' security: the role of human failure. J. Electron. Sci. Technol. 14(4), 311–318 (2016)
6. Wiercioch, A., Teufel, S., Teufel, B.: The authentication dilemma. J. Softw. 13(5), 277–286 (2018). https://doi.org/10.17706/jsw.13.5.277-286
7. Teufel, S., Teufel, B.: Crowd energy information security culture: security guidelines for smart environments. In: Proceedings of the IEEE International Conference on Smart City/SocialCom/SustainCom (SmartCity), Chengdu, China, pp. 123–128 (2015)
8. Schlienger, T., Teufel, S.: Information security culture: the socio-cultural dimension in information security management. In: Proceedings IFIP TC11 17th International Conference on Information Security: Visions and Perspectives, Cairo, Egypt, 7–9 May, 2002
9. Da Veiga, A., Eloff, J.: A framework and assessment instrument for information security culture. Comput. Secur. 29(2), 196–207 (2010)
10. Heidt, M., Gerlach, J.P., Buxmann, P.: Investigating the security divide between SME and large companies: how SME characteristics influence organizational IT security investments. Inf. Syst. Front. 21(6), 1285–1305 (2019). https://doi.org/10.1007/s10796-019-09959-1
11. Solms, R., von Niekerk, J.: From information security to cyber security. Comput. Secur. 38, 97–102 (2013)
12. Kersten, H., Klett, G., Reuter, J., Schröder, K.-W.: IT-Sicherheitsmanagement nach der neuen ISO 27001. Springer Fachmedien, Wiesbaden (2016)
13. Böhmer, W., Haufe, K., Klipper, S., Lohre, T., Rumpel, R., Witt, B.-C.: Managementsysteme für Informationssicherheit (ISMS) mit DIN EN ISO/IEC 27001 betreiben und verbessern. Beuth Verlag GmbH, Berlin (2018)
14. Deming, W.: Out of Crisis. M.I.T. Center for Advanced Engineering Study, Cambridge, USA (1982)
15. Calder, A.: ISO27001/ISO27002. IT Governance Publishing, Cambridgeshire (2018)
16. Federal Office for Information Security (BSI): BSI-Standard 200–2, IT Grundschutz Methodology. BSI, Bonn (2017). https://www.bsi.bund.de/EN/Publications/BSIStandards/BSIStandards_node.html
17. Nguyen, M.: Konzeption und modellierung eines cyber security canvas. International istitute of management in technology (iimt), University of Fribourg, Fribourg (2019)
18. National Institute of Standards and Technology (NIST): Framework for Improving Critical Infrastructure Cybersecurity. NIST, Gaithersburg, 16 April 2018
19. Scherm, E., Pietsch, G.: Organisation: Theorie, Gestaltung. Wandel. Oldenbourg Wissenschaftsverlag GmbH, München (2007)

20. Hofmann, H., Poltermann, A.: Den Wandel gemeinsam gestalten – Organisations-ent-wicklung "bottom-up" - Handreichung zur Unterstützung von Einrichtungen der beruflichen Rehabilitation. Nürnberg, Forschungsinstitut Betriebliche Bildung (f-bb) gGmbH (2017)
21. Moosbrugger, H., Kelava, A.: Testtheorie und Fragebogenkonstruktion. Springer, Heidelberg (2012)

Risk Forecasting Automation on the Basis of MEHARI

Pavel Yermalovich$^{(\boxtimes)}$ and Mohamed Mejri

Université Laval, Quebec City, Canada
Pavel.Yermalovich.1@ulaval.ca, Mohamed.Mejri@ift.ulaval.ca

Abstract. The application of various risk assessing benchmarks helps to identify only the current risk value. Nevertheless, the actual risk level may exceed the established indicator. Let us not forget that sometimes, the risk analysis takes too much time and establishes already outdated risk values. In this article, we will continue reviewing the issue of obtaining real-time risk values. For this, we will introduce the automated risk analysis method, which will help to reveal the risk value at any time point. This method forms the basis for predicting the probability of a targeted cyberattack [17]. The established risk level will help to optimize the information security budget and redistribute it to strengthen the most vulnerable areas.

Keywords: Risk assessment · MEHARI · Threat assessment · Vulnerability assessment · Risk prediction · Information security · Cybersecurity · Risk management · Cloud risk · Data security

1 Introduction

1.1 Motivation

Many countries create their own benchmarks based on security standards. The most popular mid-range benchmarks: ISO/IEC 270XX, COBIT 5, BSI-Standard, NIST SP 800-XX, NERC CIP-XXX, MEHARI, EBIOS Risk Manager, etc.

These benchmarks refer to each other or provide the most efficient information security criteria. Some countries use a combination of various standards to assess information security, for example, *Minimum ICT standard* [7]. It suggests the application of the following actions to assess the risk level (ID.RA) [4]:

- ID.RA-1: Identification (technical) of assets' **vulnerabilities** and their documentation.
- ID.RA-2: Regular intelligence sharing (fora and other bodies) to stay updated about cybersecurity **threats**.
- ID.RA-3: Identification and documentation of internal and external cybersecurity threats.
- ID.RA-4: Identification of possible business **impact** as a result of cybersecurity threat(s), and prediction (calculation) of the **probability** of their occurring.

H. Venter et al. (Eds.): ISSA 2020, CCIS 1339, pp. 34–49, 2020.
https://doi.org/10.1007/978-3-030-66039-0_3

– ID.RA-5: Ranging the organization's **risks** based on the impact which the threats might cause.
– ID.RA-6: Determination of possible immediate **responses** in case of a risk, prioritization of these response measures.

This list of actions is usually a part of all existing approaches to risk analysis. Scientific trends consider comparisons of various risk analysis techniques and benchmarks. However, not much attention is paid to automation and risk prediction issues. To fill this gap, we decided to consider the automation of risk forecasting on the basis of MEHARI with the subsequent possibility of connecting a risk prediction module based on the formalization of the prediction problem [16].

1.2   Our Contributions

– Real-time automated risk level assessment.
– Connection of external databases to identify the values of threats and vulnerabilities.
– Risk prediction approach.

The rest of the paper is organized as follows: Sect. 2 provides the Harmonized Method of Risk Analysis. Section 3 represents the Proposed method. Section 4 represents the Experiment result. Section 5 represents the Related work. Section 6 presents a summary of ideas aimed at practical applications in information security systems [11].

2   Background Information

2.1   Harmonized Method of Risk Analysis

MEHARI (fr. MÉthode Harmonisée d'Analyse des RIsques) - Harmonized Method of Risk Analysis comprising 4 versions of information risk analysis [6] (sorted in descending order based on analysis complexity): Expert, Standard, Pro, Manager. The risk assessment scheme proposed by MEHARI Expert is presented in Fig. 1. Only Expert, Standard, Pro versions integrate diagnostic questionnaires and use a single approach with different levels of detail (for different analysis times, complexity and budget). They are visualized in Table 1.

This approach aims at establishing an acceptable risk level. To ensure an adequate protection level, each time we need to determine what should be protected and from whom. For this, it is necessary to identify the assets and obtain information about them. The above-mentioned statement could be illustrated by the following example:

1. Analysis of business activities or processes:
    – Determining the ownership of an asset in the business process.
    – Asset analysis (assessing importance and level of each lost value).

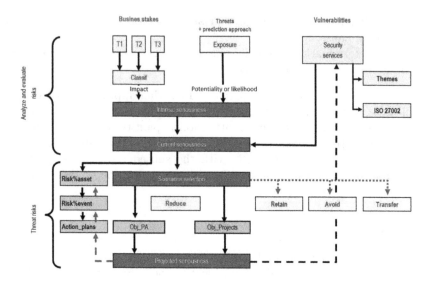

Fig. 1. Graphical structural representation of MEHARI Expert [5]

Table 1. Content comparison in various MEHARI versions

MEHARI	MEHARI		
Assessment Questionnaire	Pro	Standard	Expert
Organization of Security	+	+	+
Sites Security	+	+	+
Security of Premises			+
Wide-area Network			+
Local Area Network			+
Network Operations			+
Systems' Security and Architecture	+	+	+
IT Production Environment	+		+
Application Security	+	+	+
Security of Application Projects and Developments		+	+
Protection of Users' Work Equipment	+	+	+
Telecommunications Operations			+
Management Processes		+	+
Information Security Management			+

Given: List of business activities.

Find: Intrinsic Impact table.

2. Audit of the protection techniques applied to ensure the safety of assets:
   - Defence system analysis.
   - Risk analysis.

Given: List of protection techniques applied to ensure the safety of assets.

Find: Description of risk scenarios, risk per asset type, risk per event type. Summaries of the seriousness of scenarios.

3. Preparation of risk mitigation measures:
   - Action plans.
   - Summary of security objectives for action plans.
   - Objectives for risk reduction projects.

Given: Summary of seriousness of scenarios.

Find: List of protection techniques to ensure the safety of assets within the acceptable risk level.

This approach does not consider risk prediction but estimates the risk based on the data collected over time. The conduct of risk assessment with the MEHARI Expert tool [5] may take more than six months [16]. From this, it follows that in the context of such a risk assessment model, there are periods that remain uncontrolled. An example of such a case is shown in Fig. 2. In this graph, red horizontal bars represent an acceptable risk limit. Green bars represent the actual risk value and grey dots stand for the calculated risk values (calculations are carried out every four time units). The red vertical line indicates the periods that remain uncontrolled. Sometimes an action plan can help to reduce the risk level considerably in comparison with the established value. This can be observed when the risk level is reduced from orange to green. However, in reality, it has decreased from red to green.

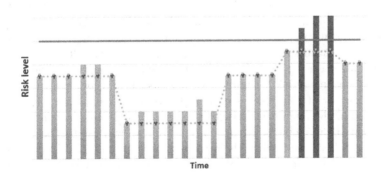

Fig. 2. Graphical representation of risks taking the passed calculated values (Color figure online)

3   Proposed Method

It is recommended to use Eq. (1) to calculate the risk level:

$$R = P \cdot I \tag{1}$$

where R is the risk value, P is the probability of an asset loss due to an attack event and I is the impact (a likely consequence) of an attack event. We are considering an attack as part of an information security incident.

Let us rewrite Eq. (1) considering the probability of the asset loss as a result of a possible attack to one of the assets with the traditional security areas of concern: confidentiality, integrity, and availability:

$$R_{asset}(Attacks)$$

$$= \sum_{i=1}^{n} \Big(P_{availability}(attack_i) \cdot I_{availability}(attack_i);$$

$$P_{integrity}(attack_i) \cdot I_{integrity}(attack_i);$$

$$P_{confidentiality}(attack_i) \cdot I_{confidentiality}(attack_i) \Big) \tag{2}$$

where $R_{asset}(Attacks)$ is a risk value due to an attack event, $P_{availability}(attack_i)$ is a probability of the asset's availability loss due to an attack event $attack_i$ and $I_{availability}(attack_i)$ is the impact (a likely consequence) of an attack event $attack_i$. On the asset's availability loss. The same applies to the asset's integrity and confidentiality due to an attack event. The number of attacks is expressed by n.

The risk assessment scheme proposed by MEHARI Expert is presented in Fig. 3.

In this approach, the decomposition of risk [15] into components is considered only for the organization of information security. However, the real probability of a threat is overlooked, since MEHARI employs only default threat values (Standard CLUSIF) and does not rely on real-time threat assessment outcomes. It is also important to carry out an assessment of assets over time. The categorization of certain information assets is sensitive to the "time" factor. An information asset can be viewed as highly confidential at a given period of time, while it may become public thereafter. In this case, it is recommended to review the categorization of this asset according to its life cycle stages. More details are described in the referenced article in section *Impact based on the contextual approach* [15]. To implement threat analysis [12], we will use the best practices of predicting cyberattacks through threat activity analysis [18]. To do this, it is necessary to decompose the probability of risk into the following components: attack, threat, vulnerability, attack vector, defense system and its quality. The graphical representation of decomposition is shown in Fig. 4.

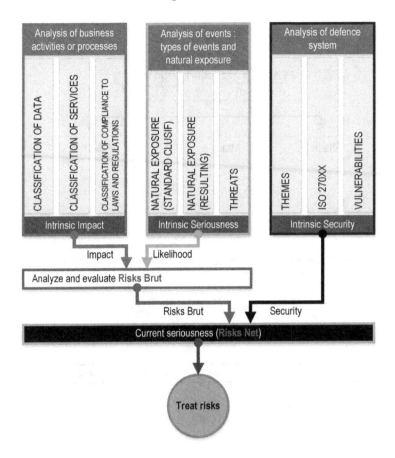

Fig. 3. Risk assessment scheme proposed by MEHARI Expert

3.1 Attacks

We can present the likelihood of an attack (ai) for all the attacks A on one of the assets for each security principle (availability, integrity or confidentiality) as follows:

$$P(A) = \sum_{i=0}^{k} \Big(P(A|a_i) \cdot P(a_i) \Big) \tag{3}$$

where,

- $P(A|a_i)$ - the likelihood of an attack (a_i) in general cyberattack statistics [3].
- $P(a_i)$ - the likelihood of an attack (a_i), Eq. (4) is used.

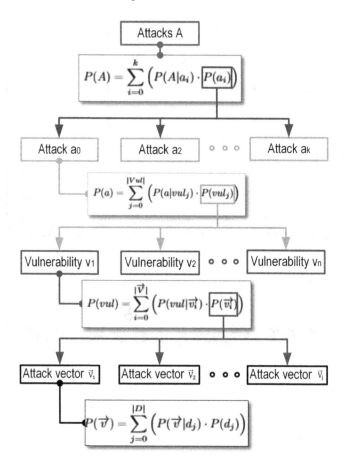

Fig. 4. Attack probability decomposition: exploiting the existing vulnerability using an attack vector

Let us analyze the lower level to determine the likelihood of an attack a through exploiting vulnerabilities Vul.

$$P(a) = \sum_{j=1}^{|Vul|} \Big(P(a|vul_j) \cdot P(vul_j) \Big) \tag{4}$$

where,

- $|Vul|$ - number of vulnerabilities enabling commitment of an attack a.
- $P(a|vul_j)$ - likelihood of an attack a occurring in the presence of a threat of exploiting a vulnerability vul_j. Equation (5) is used to determine the threats.
- $P(vul_j)$ - probability of occurrence of the vulnerability vul_j event presented in Eq. (6).

3.2 Threats

Equation (5) is used to determine the threats.

$$P(a|vul_j) = \text{``Threat Motivation''} \times \text{``Threat Capability''} \times \text{``Size''} \tag{5}$$

where,

– Threat Motivation [9] - assesses the motivation [18] of a particular group of threat agents to find and exploit the vulnerability.
– Threat Capability [10] - probable level of resistance that a threat agent [18] is capable to demonstrate against an asset.
– Size [9] - describes threat agents' characteristics (developers, system administrators, intranet users, partners, authenticated users, anonymous Internet users).

3.3 Vulnerabilities

The probability of occurrence of a vulnerability vul_j event presented in Eq. (4) depends on the total probability of exploitation of attacks vectors $\overrightarrow{V}$ presented in Eq. (6).

$$P(vul) = \sum_{i=0}^{|\overrightarrow{V}|} \left(P(vul|\overrightarrow{v_i}) \cdot P(\overrightarrow{v_i}) \right) \tag{6}$$

where,

– $|\overrightarrow{V}|$ - identifies the number of vulnerabilities vul for the attack a;
– $P(vul|\overrightarrow{v_i})$ - exploitability of a vulnerability using an attack vector $\overrightarrow{v_i}$ from the variety of attack vectors for the vulnerability vul, $P(vul|\overrightarrow{v_i})$ presented in Eq. (7). The exploitation of vulnerability in the presence of a chance to exploit it through a certain method by the attack vector.
– $P(\overrightarrow{v_i})$ - attack vector probability, can be tracked by analyzing Eq. (8).

3.4 Exploitability

In other words, $P(vul|\overrightarrow{v_i})$ indicates the exploitation of a vulnerability in the presence of a chance to exploit it through a certain method by the attack vector. The following formula is used by us to determine the exploitability:

$$\begin{aligned} P(vul|\overrightarrow{v_i}) = &\text{``Attack Vector''} \times \text{``Attack Complexity''} \\ &\times \text{``Privileges required''} \times \text{``User Interaction''} \\ &\times \text{``Exploit code maturity''} \times \text{``Easy of Discovery''} \end{aligned} \tag{7}$$

where,

– Attack Vector [2] - Common Vulnerability Scoring System (CVSS) metric reflecting the context in which it is possible to exploit the vulnerability.

- Attack Complexity [2] - CVSS metric describing the conditions beyond the attacker's control that must be created to exploit the vulnerability.
- Privileges required [2] - CVSS metric describing the level of privileges an attacker must possess before successfully exploiting the vulnerability.
- User Interaction [2] - CVSS metric capturing the requirement for a human user, other than an attacker, to participate in the successful compromise of the vulnerable component.
- Exploit code maturity [2] - CVSS metric measuring the likelihood of the vulnerability being attacked. It is typically based on the current state of exploit techniques, exploit code availability, or active "in-the-wild" exploitation. Public availability of easy-to-use exploit code increases the number of potential attackers by including those who are unskilled, thereby increasing the severity of the vulnerability.
- Easy of Discovery [9] - describes the degree of easiness for a group of threat agents targeting a particular vulnerability to get access to it (practically impossible, difficult, easy, automated tools available).

3.5   Attack Vectors

Consider the formula for the probability of an attack vector (8), the result of which is used in Eq. (6).

$$P(\overrightarrow{v}) = \sum_{j=1}^{|D|} \left(P(\overrightarrow{v}|d_j) \cdot P(d_j) \right) \tag{8}$$

where,

- $|D|$ - number of protective measures against the attack vector $\overrightarrow{v}$. We are analyzing individual protection components D in isolation, however, it is very important to consider different sets of protection components and their configuration and interactions.
- $P(\overrightarrow{v}|d_j)$ - damage caused by an attack vector $\overrightarrow{v}$ with valid protection measures d_j (return value of quality of protection against an attack vector) and statistical data.
- $P(d_j)$ - probability of applying this protection measure (yes or no)

For simplicity purposes, the component of formula $P(\overrightarrow{v}|d_j)$ is visualized in Table 2.

Based on the above decomposition of probability, the MEHARI scheme can be presented as shown in Fig. 5. Changes are highlighted in bold.

Thus, we managed to automate the receipt of the following data: prediction of the probability of threats [18], vulnerability analysis (CVSS, OWASP), security analysis.

The evaluation of the proposed approach by an example of simplified website administration on a Cloud Dedicated Server presented in Section VI in the follow article [17]. Figure 6 illustrates an example of a simplified website administration on a Cloud Dedicated Server.

Table 2. Visualization of component $P(\overrightarrow{v}|d_j)$

	$\overrightarrow{v_1}$	$\overrightarrow{v_2}$	...	$\overrightarrow{v_i}$	...	$\overrightarrow{v_{|V|}}$
d_1	$P(\overrightarrow{v_1}|d_1)$	$P(\overrightarrow{v_2}|d_1)$				
d_2	$P(\overrightarrow{v_1}|d_2)$	$P(\overrightarrow{v_2}|d_2)$				
...						
d_j				$P(\overrightarrow{v_i}|d_j)$		
...						
$d_{|D|}$						$P(\overrightarrow{v_{|V|}}|d_{|D|})$

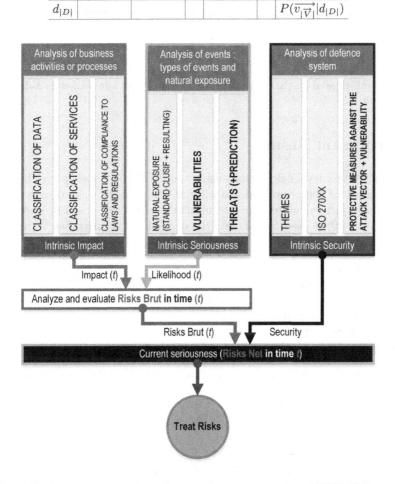

Fig. 5. Risk assessment and prediction scheme proposed by MEHARI Expert

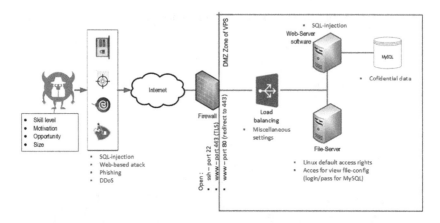

Fig. 6. Example based on the administration of an Internet site hosted on a dedicated virtual server [15]

4   Experiment Result

We conducted risk level calculations using the MEHARI Excel spreadsheets [5]. The estimation of the organizational information security was not carried out. Thus, we have just calculated the information security risk posed by operations. The full list of tables used to calculate the operational security risk is presented below:

- Wide-area Network;
- Local Area Network;
- Security and Architecture of Systems;
- IT Production Environment;
- Application Security;
- Protection of users' work equipment.

To calculate the quality of the protection service, MEHARI uses the following Eq. (9):

$$Q = 4 \cdot \frac{\sum(\lambda_i \cdot x_i)}{\sum(\lambda_i)} \tag{9}$$

where,

- x_i - Indicator of security availability service Yes (1) or lack thereof or No (0).
- λ_i - Capacity of this security system to provide proper protection in case of risk. λ_i can take four values from one to four ($\lambda_i = 1, .., 4$). These values are already predefined for each of information security assessment question.

In our calculation, we use auto-renewable values of the security service quality. This approach was already considered in Sect. 3.5. In this work, we evaluated our New approach to the security level establishment by comparing it with the

MEHARI approach in a course of determining the speed of security level establishment for an IT-company with 1,000 employees. The conducted operations and findings are presented in Fig. 7.

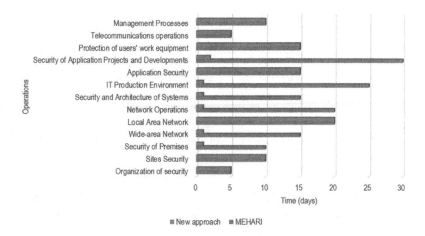

Fig. 7. Security level determining speed: New approach versus MEHARI

The optimization of risk calculation helps to save more time and redistribute it to the subsequent activities aimed at mitigating the consequences of a risk. Our approach significantly reduces time expenditures and offers an opportunity to rebuild the defense system in the best way to repel impending attacks.

5 Related Work

In the existing works, the authors [13] describe the risk assessment process via a Method for Information Security Risk Assessment based on the Dynamic Bayesian Network. The main point is the use of the Bayesian Formula to calculate the risk level. The main input parameters of this work are shown in Fig. 8.

The application of the Dynamic Bayesian Network formula for risk calculation improves the efficiency of this method. However, the authors admit the following shortcoming of this approach: *the limited input data, as well as the conditional probability tables in the mentioned model, are based on expert experience, which is characterized by definite subjectivity.* In this paper, we went further and identified key inputs for determining a risk. In addition to this we demonstrated [14] the possibility of automating the entry of this data from external knowledge bases [1]. The method proposed by OWASP (presented in Sect. 5.1) can predict risk based on an expert analysis of probability and impact. This method employs the mathematical decomposition of probability and impact to obtain a numerical value of risk. The disadvantage of this method is the lack of automation at the stage of obtaining the information from existing databases,

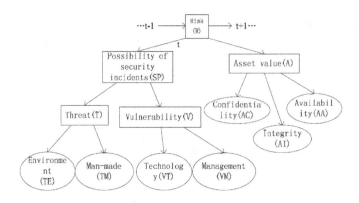

Fig. 8. Information security risk assessment model based on dynamic bayesian networks [13]

such as CVSS. However, this method is not complicated. It employs a universal risk calculator, which can be managed by anyone after a brief training.

5.1 OWASP Risk Rating Methodology

The Risk Rating Calculator [8] is based on The Open Web Application Security Project's (OWASP) Risk Rating Methodology [9]. The simplest risk calculation is presented by OWASP. All indicators are selected by the expert method, in which case there may be a human error, since this method is based on the experience of a risk assessment expert. It is a fast and simple risk assessment method. The OWASP approach presented here is based on standard methodologies and customized for the application security with the standard risk model presented in Eq. (10):

$$Risk = Likelihood \cdot Impact \tag{10}$$

The tester needs to gather information about the involved threat agent [18], the planned attack, the forecasted vulnerability, and the impact of the exploit on business. Thus, each factor has a set of options, and each option can be assigned a likelihood/impact score ranging from low = 0 level to high = 9 level.

1. The final *likelihood* score is determined by the following factors:
   - Threat agent factors [0..9]:
     (a) Level of skills [0..9].
     (b) Motivation [0..9].
     (c) Opportunity [0..9].
     (d) Size [0..9].
   - Vulnerability factors [0..9]:
     (a) Ease of discovery [0..9].
     (b) Ease of exploit [0..9].
     (c) Awareness [0..9].
     (d) Intrusion detection [0..9].

Given: Levels of threat and vulnerability factors.
Find: Estimated likelihood level [0..9].

2. Factors for estimating *impact* level:
   - Technical impact factors [0..9]:
     (a) Confidentiality loss [0..9].
     (b) Integrity loss [0..9].
     (c) Availability loss [0..9].
     (d) Accountability loss [0..9].
   - Business impact factors [0..9]:
     (a) Financial damage [0..9].
     (b) Reputation damage [0..9].
     (c) Non-compliance [0..9].
     (d) Privacy violation [0..9].

Given: List of technical impact factors and business impact factors.
Find: Estimated Impact level [0..9].

It is critical to establish and adopt a risk ranking framework that is customizable for business. The probability that the produced results are matching people's perceptions about the seriousness of risk is higher in the case of a tailored model. The tester can choose different factors that better match the particular needs of the organization and assign different priorities to the options. It is recommended to compare the ratings produced by the model with ratings produced by an expert team to ensure the priority assignment accuracy. The above-presented model assumes that all factors are equally important. At the same time, while assessing these factors, we may establish those that would be more relevant for the specific business.

5.2 Quantitative CVSS-Based Cyber Security Risk Assessment Methodology

The Vulnerability Assessment Method for The Common Vulnerability Scoring System (CVSS) [2] is a similar evaluation method relying on actual numbers. This means that the actual characteristics are established by numbers and do not depend on the approximate amount of values. A quantitative CVSS-based cyber security risk assessment methodology for IT systems [10] is an open framework for communicating the characteristics and severity of vulnerabilities. The CVSS should not be used alone for risk assessment. The Base metrics produce a score ranging from 0 to 10, which can then be modified by the score of the Temporal and Environmental metrics. Its outputs include a numerical score indicating the severity of vulnerability relative to other vulnerabilities. The detailed description of metric groups is presented in [2].

6   Conclusion

This work will significantly contribute to the improvement and modification of the existing risk analysis methods. The automatic collection of data from various sources (connection of external databases to identify the values of threats and vulnerabilities) forms the basis of the risk level automation and decreases the duration of risk analysis (real-time automated risk level assessment). The article offers ideas for modifying the MEHARI approach as an example. The risk forecasting possibility coupled with the capacity to verify the risk value at any period is essential for ensuring proper information security budgeting. Therefore, this work is emphasizing one of the key trends in the field of risk analysis, namely risk level forecasting (risk prediction approach).

References

1. Common attack pattern enumeration and classification. http://bit.ly/37s4xlo. Accessed 13 Dec 2020
2. Common vulnerability scoring system v3.1: User guide. https://bit.ly/33JM6HK. Accessed 18 Oct 2019
3. Hackmageddon. information security timelines and statistics. cyber attacks statistics: Motivations behind attacks, attack techniques, targets. https://bit.ly/2ohjjuT. Accessed 05 Oct 2019
4. Ict-minimum-standard - assessment tool (xls, 1 mb, 27.08.2018). https://bit.ly/2QyT6CR. Accessed 20 Mar 2020
5. Mehari expert (2010) rm tool. http://bit.ly/2uHDFgh. Accessed 31 Mar 2019
6. Mehari's versions. http://bit.ly/2nZ9hOT. Accessed 02 Oct 2019
7. Minimum ict standard. https://bit.ly/2QyT6CR. Accessed 20 Mar 2020
8. Owasp risk rating calculator. https://bit.ly/2VmPUij. Accessed 07 May 2019
9. Owasp risk rating methodology. http://bit.ly/2pp496W. Accessed 02 Oct 2019
10. Aksu, M.U., Dilek, M.H., Tatlı, E.İ., Bicakci, K., Dirik, H.I., Demirezen, M.U., Aykır, T.: A quantitative CVSS-based cyber security risk assessment methodology for it systems. In: 2017 International Carnahan Conference on Security Technology (ICCST), pp. 1–8. IEEE (2017)
11. Cavusoglu, H., Mishra, B., Raghunathan, S.: A model for evaluating it security investments. Commun. ACM **47**(7), 87–92 (2004)
12. Farahani, G.J., Kachoee, M.H.A., Kachoee, M.A.A.: Vulnerability assessment of the critical infrastructure against man-made threats. Ind. Eng. Manag. Syst. **17**(1), 136–145 (2018)
13. Wang, J., Fan, K., Mo, W., Xu, D.: A method for information security risk assessment based on the dynamic bayesian network. In: 2016 International Conference on Networking and Network Applications (NaNA), pp. 279–283. IEEE (2016)
14. Yermalovich, P.: Dashboard visualization techniques in information security. In: 2020 International Symposium on Networks, Computers and Communications (ISNCC), Montreal, Canada, October 2020
15. Yermalovich, P., Mejri, M.: Information security risk assessment based on decomposition probability via bayesian network. In: 2020 International Symposium on Networks, Computers and Communications (ISNCC). Montreal, Canada, October 2020

16. Yermalovich, P., Mejri, M.: Formalization of attack prediction problem. In: 2018 IEEE International Conference "Quality Management, Transport and Information Security, Information Technologies" (IT&QM&IS), pp. 280–286. IEEE (2018)
17. Yermalovich, P., Mejri, M.: Determining the probability of cyberattacks. Eur. J. Eng. Formal Sci. **4**(1), 46–63 (2020)
18. Yermalovich, P., Mejri, M.: Ontology-based model for security assessment: Predicting cyberattacks through threat activity analysis. Int. J. Network Secur. Appl. (IJNSA) **12** (2020)

Protecting Personal Data Within a South African Organisation

Mitesh Singh$^{(\boxtimes)}$, Colin Pilkington$^{(\boxtimes)}$, and Wynand van Staden

University of South Africa, Florida Park, Pretoria, South Africa
`mitesh.singh@live.co.za`, `pilkic1@unisa.ac.za`, `wynand@protonmail.com`

Abstract. The world has entered the Information Age, and the biggest contributor to this evolution is the growing ubiquity of computing. Computing technologies have transformed to a point where society can access copious amounts of information at the touch of a button, almost anywhere in the world and at any time. This access to information has raised new questions and concerns regarding privacy and the organisations that have access to personal information. One of the concerns, which is frequently highlighted in literature regarding information security, is the protection of personal information and data privacy. The purpose of this research is to explore and analyse the applications, tools, techniques and systems a South African organisation has implemented in its security frameworks to govern data privacy as well as protect personal information. To verify the effectiveness of these security frameworks, the applications, tools, techniques and systems are compared to the Protection of Personal Information Act. A hybrid analysis (using qualitative and quantitative methods) of an organisation is done by means of a case study to verify how personal information is used by their employees and if the systems and applications that contain personal information control the access to this data and prevent misuse. It was found that the organisation largely protected personal data as required.

Keywords: Information security · Data privacy · Personal information · Protection of personal information · Privacy techniques

1 Introduction

We live in a world that is surrounded by technology, which either directly or indirectly influences people. Technological advancements, especially in information systems and communications, are growing exponentially, which means that it has an increasing impact on society. People become more dependent and reliant on information and communication technologies (ICTs) as it has the ability to enhance their lives. Most aspects of our working, social, and personal lives are integrated with computing technologies and as a result of the growing ubiquity of computing, concerns are being raised regarding privacy, as well as the unethical use of personal information and private data.

© Springer Nature Switzerland AG 2020
H. Venter et al. (Eds.): ISSA 2020, CCIS 1339, pp. 50–64, 2020.
https://doi.org/10.1007/978-3-030-66039-0_4

The main focus of this research is to identify how technologies, systems, and processes are currently used to protect personal information and what privacy enhancing technologies can be incorporated by organisations to ensure data privacy. The efficacy of the practices used to collect, store, and distribute personal data will be considered, as well as comparing them to the Protection of Personal Information Act (POPIA) [13]. This research aims to address the following questions:

- How is personal information handled and managed in the organisation?
- Who should have access to personal information and private data?
- Does the organisation distribute personal information or private data?
- Are there processes, policies, systems, and technologies in place to enhance privacy and protect personal information?

A case study was conducted in a fast-moving consumer goods (FMCG) organisation to verify if personal information obtained from customers is protected, and if systems and technologies are in place to keep data private as well as enhance the protection of personal information.

The remainder of this paper is set out as follows: In Sect. 2, we discuss the privacy problem and recognise the need for privacy, providing some guidelines on protecting personal information. Privacy-enhancing technologies (PETs) and design strategies, which can be incorporated to protect private data, are explored. Section 3 discusses the case study approach and data collection methods used. The data collected is then analysed in Sect. 4 and the results presented. Finally, Sect. 5 provides concluding remarks.

2   Background Literature

Over the last few years, many information technology (IT) solution services and products have made their way into the industry's marketplace and the number of new services and products is growing exponentially. These applications capture large amounts of data pertaining to a business as well as its users [12]. Organisations collect and store data for record keeping and contact purposes, allowing them to access customer information for operational requirements. This data, which will often contain information such as biographical details, contact numbers, addresses, identity numbers, and in some cases bank account information, is required to service customers. This data can also be processed and aggregated to extract business insights, which may lead to privacy issues [12].

2.1   The Privacy Problem and the Need for Privacy

The evolution of technology has placed society in The Information Age, which has led to information and communication processes becoming the driving force of social evolution in our daily lives [10]. This evolution combined with the ubiquity of computing, has led to privacy concerns and the protection of personal information is gaining more attention. The ease of access to data poses a challenge in protecting information which is of a private and personal nature. The Internet of Things (IoT), coupled with Big Data systems, allows for the collection of enormous amounts of personal, private data, leading to an increase in the volume and detail of data that organisations collect [8]. This data is used to generate benefits for the organisation that can sometimes lead to confidentiality issues, especially when private information about a person is used without their knowledge or consent.

As users start accepting and using different technologies for interacting and transacting, they provide more personal information to access richer experiences and this makes them more susceptible to privacy and security threats [9]. However, as social beings, we need norms, customs, rules, and conventions that allow us to co-exist, collaborate, and prosper [16]. Not having these codes of conduct, including security systems, allows for the misuse of information and data privacy to be ignored.

Privacy concerns are raised when organisations that acquire, store and process data, such as personal information, use this information in an unwanted, intrusive, or invasive way and may even cause harm. Information security, privileged user access, and regulatory compliance have been identified as some of the important risks inherent in cloud computing [2], and a survey exploring the ethical and social consequences of computing found that privacy was the most dominant issue that far outweighed any other issues included in the survey [18]. Examples of attacks include account and credential hijacking, which enables an attacker to access a person's cloud services, track his or her activities, manipulate data, and perform exploitative acts, causing reputational damage and financial loss [2]. Another issue is customer segmentation, where companies divide their potential customers into groups that share similar characteristics, which can lead to people being excluded from services based on potentially distorted judgments [15]. Notably, information security was rated as the top threat in interviews with South African participants [3].

The problem lies in what is considered to be adequate when it comes to data protection by organisations that collect, store, and process personal information. Additionally, which systems, policies, or privacy enhancing technologies are available to protect information that is private and personal?

2.2   Keeping Private Data and Personal Information Protected

To protect against undesirable use and misuse of information, particularly confidential information, some governments have implemented data protection laws requiring regulatory compliance from organisations. Regulatory compliance with a law or act such as POPIA requires organisations to provide sufficient data security and protection of personal information. POPIA recognises that everyone has the right to privacy and that this right includes the right to protection against the unlawful collection, retention, dissemination, and use of personal information [13]. The Act refers to eight conditions for the lawful processing of personal

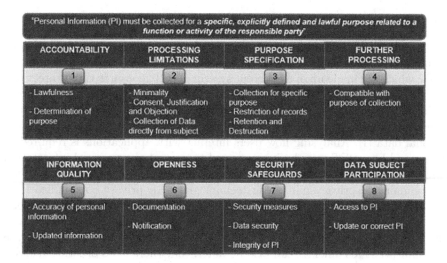

"Personal Information (PI) must be collected for a **specific, explicitly defined and lawful purpose related to a function or activity of the responsible party**"			
ACCOUNTABILITY	**PROCESSING LIMITATIONS**	**PURPOSE SPECIFICATION**	**FURTHER PROCESSING**
1	2	3	4
- Lawfulness - Determination of purpose	- Minimality - Consent, Justification and Objection - Collection of Data directly from subject	- Collection for specific purpose - Restriction of records - Retention and Destruction	- Compatible with purpose of collection
INFORMATION QUALITY	**OPENNESS**	**SECURITY SAFEGUARDS**	**DATA SUBJECT PARTICIPATION**
5	6	7	8
- Accuracy of personal information - Updated information	- Documentation - Notification	- Security measures - Data security - Integrity of PI	- Access to PI - Update or correct PI

Fig. 1. The eight conditions for the lawful processing of personal information.

information, which are summarised in Fig. 1. Acts such as POPIA indicate the significance of protecting personal information and data privacy.

When assessing the need for identifiable data during the course of a transaction, the first key question is: how much personal information or data is truly required for the proper functioning of the information system involving this transaction [5]? Thus, privacy risk analysis and management is used to create privacy risk models, which can be used as tools to help system designers identify, understand, and prioritise privacy risks for specific applications [7]. Additionally, increased or improper access due to lack of security controls may lead to carelessness when protecting stored information [14]. Verifying the identity of the person accessing information can be incorporated into a system via user profile controls, role security, and privileges assigned to specific users, while being able to connect information accessibility to specific individuals can be used to limit unauthorised access attempts. Alongside access control are techniques such as cryptography, anonymisation, privacy-preserving queries and differential privacy that can be used by organisations to protect private data [8]. These techniques are useful for protecting the confidentiality of sensitive data.

A critical review of information systems, processes, and technologies will need to be done continually, which may mean a fundamental re-evaluation of the very nature of the technologies we use and how we use them [17]. It is, therefore, considered important to have security as well as privacy enhancing systems incorporated into the information technology and computing realm.

2.3   Privacy-Enhancing Technologies (PET)

Privacy-enhancing technologies (PETs) are being implemented by organisations in an attempt to provide systematic protection of consumers' personal data [4]. PETs, which are made up of a coherent system of ICT measures that protect privacy by eliminating or reducing personal data or by preventing unnecessary processing of personal data (without losing functionality of the information system), have been developed over the years in order to help protect internally stored personal data [1]. Analysing how users interact with applications is required to understand how PETs can be incorporated to protect the personal information stored in these applications. A proposed privacy architecture (Fig. 2) identifies four domains of privacy enhancing technologies [11]: private communications, personal control, identity management and organisational safeguards. The private communication channel covers the entire span of solutions but does not imply that all (or even many) privacy solutions should share the same private communications channel. It can also be noted that there is no ordering relation (implied by the positioning of the layers) between the solutions.

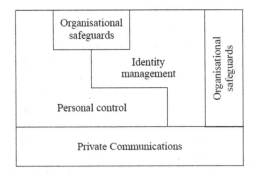

Fig. 2. Working version of the privacy architecture [11].

Privacy design strategies enable the IT developer to make well-founded privacy choices during the concept development and analysis phase of software development [6], which support privacy-by-architecture as well as privacy-by-policy approaches [15]. The eight privacy design strategies can be grouped into two classes: data-oriented and process-oriented strategies, which are linked to privacy-by-architecture and privacy-by-policy respectively. Table 1 summarises these eight design strategies, many of which can be linked to regulations such as POPIA.

For the purpose of this study, we will determine if the selected organisation incorporates any of these strategies (or something similar), either through architecture (technology) or policy, and how they implement it to enhance privacy and protect personal information.

Table 1. Privacy design strategies [6]

Type	No.	Strategy	Description
Data Orientated	1	Minimize	"The amount of personal data that is processed should be restricted to the minimal amount possible." (p. 7)
	2	Hide	"Any personal data, and their interrelationships, should be hidden from plain view." (p. 8)
	3	Separate	"Personal data should be processed in a distributed fashion, in separate compartments whenever possible." (p. 8)
	4	Aggregate	"Personal data should be processed at the highest level of aggregation and with the least possible detail in which it is (still) useful." (p. 9)
Process Orientated	5	Inform	"Data subjects should be adequately informed whenever personal data is processed." (p. 9)
	6	Control	"Data subjects should be provided agency over the processing of their personal data." (p. 9)
	7	Enforce	"A privacy policy compatible with legal requirements should be in place and should be enforced." (p. 10)
	8	Demonstrate	"Be able to demonstrate compliance with the privacy policy and any applicable legal requirements." (p. 10)

3 Design and Implementation

The research design chosen for this research was an exploratory, hybrid (qualitative and quantitative) case study approach using interpretivism as the research paradigm. Considering the research problem is focused on security and privacy within a South African organisation, a case study provides a good approach to obtaining insight into the technologies utilised and implemented in an organisation to enhance privacy. System and application analysis and reviews, survey questionnaires with employees, and field observations were performed as the research methods to collect data. Ethics clearance was obtained from the relevant research ethics committee.

3.1 Data Collection

Three departments of an FMCG organisation that would generally need to use personal information were chosen: the Master Data department, the Credit department, and the Customer Interaction Centre. A sample size of five employees from each department was used, made up of a manager, a supervisor, and three clerks for each department. The participants were overtly observed carrying out their daily tasks to investigate how personal information is acquired, accessed, and what it is used for. The field notes included what data was accessible, whether the data was distributed, and whether data privacy was maintained.

Surveys were conducted with the same 15 employees in the form of closed-ended questions to determine what private data or personal information is accessible to them, what it is used for, and whether they are aware of organisation or government data privacy regulations such as POPIA. Questions regarding who has authorisation to view and distribute personal information were also asked. The questionnaires were distributed using the online web-based application SoGoSurvey (https://www.sogosurvey.com), and the responses captured in a Microsoft Excel spreadsheet for analysis.

System and application reviews were conducted, looking at how data is input, stored, read, and archived, as well as if access control, authorisations, and privileges functionality was available and enabled to enhance privacy. Three main systems or applications were identified in this study, namely: the Enterprise Resource Planning (ERP) system, the Customer Relationship Management (CRM) system and the Centralised Database Management (CDM) application. To validate the effectiveness of protecting personal information and keeping data private, the systematic processes were also compared to POPIA to validate compliance as well as identify gaps or weaknesses.

4   Research Results and Discussion

4.1   Master Data Department

An analysis of the processes regarding acquiring, creating, reading, updating, and deleting of personal information in the organisation was conducted. Two main processes were identified, which related to the managing of customers' personal information: creation and maintenance. It was observed that the two processes are initiated by employees internal to the organisation from the different departments or functions.

New business development managers request new customers to be created by logging on to the CDM application, which is a web-based workflow application, and completing an online form as well as submitting a completed and signed application form (scanned in pdf format). The signed application form, contains the following personal information (which was completed by the customer): title, name, surname, identity number, company registration number, VAT registration number, store address, home address, mobile phone number, store phone number, home phone number, fax number, email address, bank account information (if customer requires a credit facility), marital status, if married in community of property, then spousal information (title, name, surname, identity number) is required. By signing the form, consent (documented in the terms and conditions) is given to the organisation to utilise that personal information in order to provide the customer with products and services.

Account managers, sales managers and distribution personnel (drivers, logistics managers, and route planners) initiate maintenance requests after engaging with customers on a regular basis. They only have access to log maintenance requests on the CDM application.

Personnel from the centralised Master Data department then capture the information received via the CDM application into the ERP system. The Master Data employees all had access to read and write (view and create/maintain) all attributes of personal information in the ERP system but only read access from the CDM application. They could only extract data from the CDM application, but not edit the data they extracted.

4.2   The Customer Interaction Centre (CIC)

Once the data is captured (created or maintained) in the ERP system, the CIC would use this information to provide a service (order generation) to customers. During the order generation observations, it was noted that the CIC agent used CRM (an extension of the ERP system specifically used for customer interactions) and had a limited view of the customer's master data and personal information. The only data elements that were available to the CIC agent to view were the fields that were needed to confirm the customer identity (contact information such as name, address, phone numbers, available credit, and payment terms), as well as internal organisation fields (such as the sales office and delivery location) allowing the order to be delivered. The CIC agent did not have access to the customer's identity number or banking details as the CRM system restricted what information was displayed on their order capturing screen, which is the only screen that was accessible to them.

4.3   The Credit Department

During the observations conducted in the credit department, it was noted that the credit clerks work directly on the ERP system and have access to view more customer master data information in the system than the CIC agents. They have access to view the customer's personal details such as identity number, banking details, address, company's registration details, credit bureau records, and transaction history for payments.

The credit clerks need a holistic view of a customer to verify details, such as bank information (to ensure that payments are allocated to the correct customer), legal information (such as registered company details and identity numbers), and all associated contact information. The ability for staff in the credit department to view this personal information is needed in the event the customer defaults on a payment and the debt needs to be collected either via communication attempts and, after a certain period, via a legal agency. They, however, cannot edit this information – it is read only.

4.4   Survey Questionnaire Responses

The responses to the survey questions were grouped into following categories:

- Policy and the Protection of Personal Information Act
- Accessibility to personal information
- Disclosure and distribution of personal information
- Security and opportunities for processing of personal information

The following sections expand on the results obtained from the survey questionnaires.

Table 2. Accessibility to personal information

Department	Role	Read access	Write access	Restricted access	Extract access
Master Data	Manager	Yes	Yes	No	Yes
	Supervisor	Yes	Yes	No	Yes
	Clerks	Yes	Yes	No	Yes
Credit	Manager	Yes	No	No	Yes
	Supervisor	Yes	No	No	Yes
	Clerks	Yes	No	2 Yes; 1 No	Yes
CIC	Manager	Yes	No	Yes	No
	Supervisor	Yes	No	Yes	No
	Clerks	No	No	Yes	No

Policy and the Protection of Personal Information Act. The results from the survey questions related to policy and POPIA indicate that all employees claim to be familiar with POPIA and have a good understanding of what personal information is. The results also show that all employees acknowledge that policies regarding ethics and the use of data relating to personal information exist, are proficient in the organisation's Code of Conduct and concur on what personal information is used for by the organisation, which is "To service the customer (Contact them, Ordering, Delivery, Invoicing, etc.)".

These results suggest that the organisation has introduced POPIA to their employees, but do not imply that each and every employee is well versed in the specific requirements of the Act. It is also evident that the organisation has measures in place to ensure employees adhere to the proper use of personal information by incorporating policies relating to personal information and enforcing a code of conduct. The privacy design strategies that can be associated with this are Enforce and Demonstrate as well as POPIA conditions such as Accountability, Openness and Processing Limitation.

Accessibility of Personal Information. The results from the survey questions that related to the accessibility of personal information (See Table 2) indicate that only selected employees have full access to view all of the customers' personal information: the entire Master Data department and the supervisors and managers from both the Credit department and CIC. The remaining employees have limited or restricted access to view customers' personal information (although there seems to be an inconsistency with the credit clerk role, as one of the three employees claim their access is not restricted). With regards to write or edit access, only employees from the Master Data department can create/update/maintain customers' personal information. Lastly, only employees from the Master Data and Credit departments have the ability to extract and download a customers personal information from the system. The CIC does not have the ability to download customers' personal information.

These results suggest that the organisation has built restrictions and controls into all systems and processes used by the selected employees to aid the protection of personal information and keep this data private. This supports the processes analysed and what was noted in the observations conducted. Customers' personal information fields were greyed out for the employees in the Credit department and CIC and they could not edit this information. This is also in line with the organisation's Segregation Of Duties (SOD) policy which makes it clear that a customer's personal information can and must only be created, updated and deleted by the Master Data department. SOD is managed by role and privilege administration and management embedded in the ERP, CRM and CDM systems, which only allows certain users to have certain access and functionality. There could be a gap in the SOD process as there was one employee that claims to not be restricted from accessing personal information, yet the remaining employees in that role indicate that they are. Privacy design strategies that can be associated here are 'Minimise', 'Hide' and 'Separate' as well as POPIA conditions such as 'Processesing Limitations', 'Purpose Specification' and 'Security Safeguards'.

Disclosure and Distribution of Personal Information. The results from the survey questions related to the disclosure and distribution of personal information indicate that all employees are prohibited, as per policy, from distributing customers' personal information to any person outside of the organisation. They have never had the need to share any of the organisation's customers' personal information externally and believe that they are not allowed to do so. This shows that all employees demonstrate accountability as well as knowledge and awareness of the organisation's Code of Conduct and policies relating to personal information and keeping data private (not distributing this information).

All employees also claim they are restricted by the systems they use from distributing customers' personal information to any person outside of the organisation. This is not entirely accurate as the ERP system restricts only certain employees from extracting and downloading customers' personal information. By default, if information can be extracted from the system, it can also be saved and distributed (even externally). Another contradictory factor is the use of other applications available to the employees which could be used to 'copy' information such as the 'Snipping Tool' application, but no evidence exists to suggest that this is being done from the observations and surveys conducted.

Even though distribution of personal information is still possible, the responses pertaining to disclosure and distribution of personal information suggest that the organisation utilises policies, processes and systems to aid in the protection of personal information where disclosure and distribution is concerned. If distribution of personal information is limited as well as prohibited, then this increases personal information privacy and protection. Privacy design strategies that can be associated here are 'Control' and 'Enforce' as well as POPIA conditions such as 'Processesing Limitations', 'Further Processing', 'Accountability' and 'Security Safeguards'.

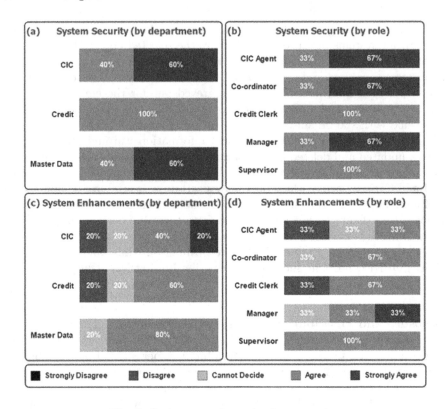

Fig. 3. System security and enhancements.

Security and Opportunities for Processing of Personal Information.
The results from the survey questions related to security with regards to the processing of personal information (see Fig. 3) are split by department and roles. Figure 3(a) indicates that all departments either agree or strongly agree that the systems used to store customers' personal information is secure. The majority of employees that strongly agree are from the CIC and Master Data department, namely the managers, CIC agents and co-ordinators (see Fig. 3(b)).

Questions related to opportunities for the processing of personal information reveal that the majority of employees agree (20% of the CIC strongly agree) that more enhancements need to be made in the systems to protect customers' personal information (see Fig. 3(c)). 20% of employees from each department cannot decide, and 20% from the CIC and Credit department disagree. Figure 3(d) indicates the actual roles where users either strongly agree, agree, disagree or cannot decide.

This contradicts the responses regarding the secureness of the systems. If the systems are believed to be secure, then enhancements would not be needed to ensure a customers' personal information is protected. The responses could also imply that the employees believe there is always room for improvement.

4.5   System and Application Analysis and Review

Investigations were carried out to identify the actual data fields which are created and maintained in the company's ERP system. The ERP system was selected as all master data and personal information is stored and referenced from there. From the analysis conducted, it was deduced that this information can be split into groups, which is dependant on the functions that process and consume this information for operations.

It was noted that employees create and maintain different master data fields for a customer record. The only employees that have privileges to create and maintain customer master data are those from the centralised Master Data department. The other departments were either blocked (could not access a customer creation or maintenance transaction code) or could only read customer master data fields (the fields were greyed out). The master data in the system, for a customer record, is separated by tabs which correspond to the specific department that would generally consume this data, for example, Sales, Distribution, Pricing, or Credit. The system then restricts access to other departments that should not have access to the information by assigning privileges to roles. This suggests that the system blocks or limits access (if the privilege is not assigned) to certain fields or tabs from employees. For example, an employee working in a sales department such as the CIC should not be able to view customer's credit information fields, such as bank information, in the system. While conducting the observations, it was noted that the CIC employees only use the CRM system, which displayed information relevant for order capturing only, limiting accessibility to personal information.

4.6   Enhancing Privacy Through Legislation and PETs

After completing the observations, surveys, and analysis of the systems and processes, the results were compared to POPIA requirements as well as the privacy design strategies relating to PETs described in Sect. 2.3. Table 3 summarises how the organisation has incorporated privacy design strategies (using PETs) and adapted their systems and processes for the lawful processing of personal information related to POPIA, showing that it adheres to POPIA requirements and the use of PETs.

Legislation, particularly POPIA, was considered in this study in order to establish conformance by the organisation and confirm that required regulatory compliance does encourage organisations to protect personal information and take measures to keep data private. The data collected from this research shows that POPIA is enforced mainly through process in this particular organisation and aids in the protection of personal information. The analysis also verifies that PETs do exist and have been implemented in the systems specific to this organisation, which assists in protecting private data.

Table 3. POPIA requirements and PET's used by the organisation

POPIA requirements	POPIA Legislation explanation	How the organisation addresses the requirement	PET design strategies applied
Consent	Personal information may only be processed if the data subject or competent person consents to the processing. (11.(1)(a))	The customer application form, which was examined during the observations contains terms and conditions regarding consent which is authorised and signed by the customer	Control
Direct marketing	Direct marketing by means of any form of electronic communication, including automatic calling machines, SMSs or e-mail is prohibited unless the data subject has given his, her, or its consent. (69.(1)(a))	From the processes analysed and what was observed, the organisation does not engage in any direct marketing activities	Demonstrate, Inform
Auto-mated decision making	Automated processing to make a decision based on a credit worthiness, reliability, location, or health profile that has legal consequences or substantial impact is not allowed. (71.(1))	Customer application forms, which were examined during the observations contain terms and conditions regarding decision making, which is authorised and signed by the customer	Inform
Records retention	Records of personal information must not be retained any longer than is necessary for achieving purpose for which the information was collected or subsequently processed. (14.(1))	The Master Data department has a CRUD process which references deleting, suppressing and archiving customer records	Mini-mise, Aggregate
Third-party processing	Collection of information from another source is necessary to maintain the legitimate interests of the responsible party or of third party to whom the information is supplied. (12.(2)(d)(v))	The customer application form, which was examined during the observations contains terms and conditions regarding delegation, sub-contracting or transferring of information, which is authorised and signed by the customer	Separate, Control, Inform
Cross-border flow	A responsible party in the Republic may not transfer personal information about a data subject to a third party who is in a foreign country. (72.(1))	The organisation studied currently only operates in South Africa and no evidence of cross border personal information transfers was noted during the observations and analysis	Control, Enforce, Demonstrate
Incidents management/Complaints	Receiving and investigating complaints about alleged violations of the protection of personal information of data subjects. (40.(1)(d)(i))	The Customer Interaction Center has a "Query, Complaints & Incidents (QCI)" process which applies to complaints	Enforce, Demonstrate

5   Conclusion

This research aims to identify how personal information is used, and if technology and security systems are available to enhance data privacy and protect personal information. In this paper, the privacy problem associated with personal information was discussed as well as some guidelines for keeping data private and protecting personal information. Demonstrating what PETs are and how they can be incorporated by organisations to protect private data, was explored. The exploratory nature of this research assists in analysing the effectiveness of the current technologies used for data privacy and information security as well as identify current gaps associated with data privacy in a South African context. The interpretations resulting from this case study, as well as the qualitative and quantitative data analysis, provide an understanding of the security mechanisms organisations incorporate to manage data privacy and protect personal information.

Insights were gained on how an organisation collects, updates, stores and makes use of personal information in order to service their customers, as well as who has access to personal information and, lastly, if this personal information is distributed outside the organisation. The results from the study show that even though some flaws or gaps do exist, organisations do incorporate PETs as well as have policies, codes of conduct, and processes implemented in order to protect personal information and keep data private.

These insights can contribute to current theories on data privacy and provide an understanding of how technology can add value to organisations as well as society regarding concerns with protecting personal information. The challenges experienced due to the misuse of information and unprotected data poses questions for privacy when using computing technology. This study corroborates how one South African organisation uses processes, systems, legislation and technologies to enhance privacy and protect private and personal data. This work can be expanded on by researching what tools, applications and techniques different organisations from different countries utilise and have incorporated into their systems and processes. By confirming that systems and privacy enhancing technologies assist in reducing the misuse of personal information, certain actions can be taken by organisations and society to ensure data privacy is maintained by acknowledging best practices for protecting personal information.

References

1. Borking, J., et al.: Handbook of Privacy and Privacy-Enhancing Technologies The case of Intelligent Software Agents, 2003 edn. College bescherming persoonsgegevens, The Hague (2003). https://doi.org/10.13140/2.1.4888.7688
2. Brender, N., Markov, I.: Risk perception and risk management in cloud computing: results from a case study of Swiss companies. Int. J. Inf. Manag. **33**(5), 726–733 (2013). https://doi.org/10.1016/j.ijinfomgt.2013.05.004
3. Carroll, M., van der Merwe, A., Kotze, P.: Secure cloud computing: benefits, risks and controls. In: 2011 Information Security for South Africa, pp. 1–9, August 2011. https://doi.org/10.1109/ISSA.2011.6027519

4. Gan, M.F., Chua, H.N., Wong, S.F.: Privacy enhancing technologies implementation: an investigation of its impact on work processes and employee perception. Telematics Inform. **38**, 13–29 (2019). https://doi.org/10.1016/j.tele.2019.01.002. http://www.sciencedirect.com/science/article/pii/S0736585318309286, https://linkinghub.elsevier.com/retrieve/pii/S0736585318309286

5. Hes, R., Borking, J.: Privacy-Enhancing Technologies: The Path to Anonymity. Registratiekamer, Den Haag (2000)

6. Hoepman, J.H.: Privacy Design Strategies. Institute for Computing and Information Sciences (ICIS), Radboud University, Nijmegen, October 2012. http://arxiv.org/abs/1210.6621

7. Hong, J.I., Ng, J.D., Lederer, S., Landay, J.A.: Privacy risk models for designing privacy-sensitive ubiquitous computing systems. In: Proceedings of the 2004 Conference on Designing Interactive Systems Processes, Practices, Methods, and Techniques - DIS 2004, p. 91. ACM Press, New York (2004). https://doi.org/10.1145/1013115.1013129

8. Moreno, J., Serrano, M., Fernández-Medina, E.: Main issues in big data security. Future Internet **8**(3), 44 (2016). https://doi.org/10.3390/fi8030044

9. Nakayama, M., Chen, C., Taylor, C.: The effects of perceived functionality and usability on privacy and security concerns about cloud application adoptions. J. Inf. Syst. Appl. Res. **5**(3), 1–23 (2017)

10. Nguyen, T.C.: Who Invented the Computer? https://www.thoughtco.com/history-of-computers-4082769. Accessed 28 Dec 2019

11. Olivier, M.S.: A layered architecture for privacy-enhancing technologies. S. Afr. Comput. J. **31**, 53–61 (2003)

12. Perera, C., Ranjan, R., Wang, L., Khan, S.U., Zomaya, A.Y.: Big data privacy in the Internet of Things era. IT Prof. **17**(3), 32–39 (2015). https://doi.org/10.1109/MITP.2015.34

13. Republic of South Africa: Protection of Personal Information, Act 4 of 2013. Government Gazette (912), pp. 1–75 (2013). http://www.gov.za/sites/www.gov.za/files/37067_26-11_Act4of2013ProtectionOfPersonalInfor_correct.pdf

14. Solove, D.J.: A taxonomy of privacy. Univ. Pennsylvania Law Rev. **154**(3), 477–560 (2006)

15. Spiekermann, S., Cranor, L.: Engineering privacy. IEEE Trans. Softw. Eng. **35**(1), 67–82 (2009). https://doi.org/10.1109/TSE.2008.88

16. Stahl, B.: Morality, ethics, and reflection: a categorization of normative IS research. J. Assoc. Inf. Syst. **13**(8), 636–656 (2012). https://doi.org/10.17705/1jais.00304

17. Stahl, B.C., Eden, G., Jirotka, M., Coeckelbergh, M.: From computer ethics to responsible research and innovation in ICT. Inf. Manag. **51**(6), 810–818 (2014). https://doi.org/10.1016/j.im.2014.01.001

18. Stahl, B.C., Timmermans, J., Mittelstadt, B.D.: The ethics of computing. ACM Comput. Surv. **48**(4), 1–38 (2016). https://doi.org/10.1145/2871196

Concern for Information Privacy in South Africa: An Empirical Study Using the OIPCI

Adéle da Veiga[(⊠)] [iD]

School of Computing, College of Science, Engineering and Technology, University of South Africa (UNISA), Florida Campus, Johannesburg, South Africa
dveiga@unisa.ac.za

Abstract. The information privacy concern of consumers concerning the processing of their personal information by online organizations (websites) is investigated in this study by means of a quantitative approach. An overview of existing concerns about information privacy instruments are presented based on a literature review. The Online Information Privacy Concern Instrument (OIPCI) is used to study consumers' expectations and experience regarding information privacy principles in order to identify their concerns about information privacy. The study was conducted in South Africa with a demographical representative sample of 1000 participants. Gaps were identified where consumers experienced that online organizations were not meeting their privacy expectations. This indicated that the regulatory requirements (in this case, the Protection of Personal Information Act (POPI) are perceived as not being met. The results indicate that while consumers in South Africa have a high expectation for privacy, it is not met in practice. Corrective action and interventions are required from a government and online organization perspective.

Keywords: Information privacy concern · Confidence · Expectations · CFIP · OIPCI · POPI

1 Introduction

Consumers are concerned about the use and protection of their personal information by organizations [1–3], specifically their financial, security and identity information [4]. In recent years, large data breaches have occurred. For example, 540 million Facebook user records were exposed in 2019; First American Financial Corporation had 885 million records exposed, including social security numbers and banking transactions; and in 2019, Microsoft leaked emails and the private contact information of 49 million Instagram users were exposed [5]. These data breaches happen due to various reasons, including internal threats, cyber criminals and exploited applications. While consumers are concerned about the security of their personal information provided to organizations, they are also increasingly concerned about the use of their information by organizations for activities such as advertising, marketing, profiling, location tracking and behavioral tracking [6].

© Springer Nature Switzerland AG 2020
H. Venter et al. (Eds.): ISSA 2020, CCIS 1339, pp. 65–80, 2020.
https://doi.org/10.1007/978-3-030-66039-0_5

Various researchers have studied consumers' concern for information privacy using different instruments in different contexts [7–12, 36]. Few studies have been conducted in South Africa to understand privacy concern. The privacy expectations and experience of online consumers in line with regulatory requirements have not yet been studied with a representative sample in SA [15]. While South Africa has a privacy law, the Protection of Personal Information Act (POPI) [13], it only came into effect as of 1 July 2020. Organizations are in the process of implementing compliance requirements, but has a one year grace period to do so [14]. Multinational organizations in South Africa have to comply with the privacy laws of other jurisdictions and therefore implement data protection requirements. At the same time, South African consumers have certain expectations of privacy and concerns about the protection of personal information.

This study aims to identify the concern for information privacy of South Africans consumers in an online context. The instrument used, the Online Information Privacy Concern Instrument (OIPCI) [15], focuses on information privacy in the context of the privacy expectations and experience of consumers about specific internationally accepted privacy principles to determine the concern for information privacy. This instrument extends the context of the initial concern for information privacy instruments to include not only the concern, but also the expectations, experience and legal requirements for privacy. This paper is structured as follows: Sect. 2 gives an overview of the concern for information privacy followed by Sect. 3 which gives an overview of information privacy concern instruments. The research methodology is discussed in Sect. 4 and the results of the survey and statistical validation of the questionnaire in Sect. 5. This is followed by the conclusion in Sect. 6.

2   Concerns About Information Privacy

The scope of this paper relates to the personal identifiable information of individuals, referred to as information privacy [16]. Personal information relates to the information of an identifiable, living, natural person; juristic persons (legal entity such as a company) are included in the laws of some jurisdictions. Examples of personal information are a person's name and surname, gender, sex, age, religion, disability, health information, identifying numbers and symbols, email addresses, blood type, biometric information, opinions, views or preferences [13]. Personal identifiable information is increasingly processed through digital means. While the processing of such information is necessary to conclude business transactions and deliver services, it raises concern among consumers – which is referred to as the "concern for information privacy (CFIP)" or the "information privacy concern (IPC)".

Concern for information privacy is understood as individuals' concern about information privacy practices [1]. With regard to the privacy concern, Gavison [17:424] states, "I argue only that privacy refers to a unique concern that should be given weight in balancing values." She refers to various concerns about information privacy, such as the way information is acquired and the relationships in which confidentiality and specifically secrecy, anonymity and solitude are referred to as "privacy" in legal terms. She categorizes concern for information privacy in two distinct areas: (i) privacy concern because an individual has insufficient privacy and (ii) unequal distribution of privacy in a societal context, which could lead to "manipulation, deception, and threats to autonomy and democracy" [17:444]. She argues that the law cannot in all circumstances compensate for privacy losses and that the outcome of court decisions might not "reflect fully or adequately the perceived need for privacy in our lives".

As individuals, we have our own concern for information privacy, which might be addressed by the law partially or not at all. By using only the law as a measure to implement privacy would mean that individual expectations for privacy is disregarded. It might well be that in some cases the law exceeds privacy expectations and in other cases it does not adequately address it, which could result in concern for information privacy for the individual. Furthermore, individuals could also be concerned about privacy where they experience that organizations do not honor the privacy requirements of the law or perhaps not their inherent expectations of privacy. There are thus two sides which must be considered when attempting to understand concern for information privacy: the one is the individual's expectation for privacy in various matters such as confidentiality, minimality, sharing of data, collection and use of data; the other is that one has to consider whether these expectations are met in reality, since if it is not, it will increase the individual's concern for privacy. Furthermore, if the privacy expectations of individuals are in line with the regulatory requirements for privacy, these must be met in practice – else the data processor is not only in contravention of the law, but also not meeting the individual's privacy expectations. This could increase the concern for information privacy and affect the trust of individuals in data processors processing their personal information [18].

The RSA survey [4] found that the concern for information privacy varied based on demographical factors and nationality, where consumers from different countries had different concerns. This study specifically focuses on understanding the information privacy concern of consumers in South Africa. The next section gives an overview of the various instruments available to measure the concern for information privacy and concludes with the instrument selected for this study.

3   Overview of CFIP Instruments

A literature search using Harzing's Publish or Perish software program was conducted to identify the top 10 most cited papers focusing on concern for information privacy. A limitation of this approach is that new research is not included. Therefore, a further search was conducted in Scopus with the date period from 2015 to 2020 to identify the most recent concern for information privacy studies. Twenty-two papers were retrieved using the keywords "information privacy concern", of which 11 were applicable after duplicates were removed. An overview of the prominent concern for information privacy studies from these searches are presented in Table 1. It includes the instruments developed by Westin as well as Smith, Milberg and Burke, who developed some of the first privacy indexes, which were adapted for various other studies identified in the search.

A number of the concern for information privacy surveys were conducted building on the work of Westin, mostly measuring the privacy concern of the individual perspective (e.g. CFIPT and IUIPC). Smith et al. [16] identified that concern for information privacy studies were conducted either from the individual's concern perspective (e.g. their personality) or from a privacy experience perspective (what the experience in practice was, such as their information being shared or exposed in the past). It was found

Table 1. Overview of prominent concern for information privacy studies using instruments.

Instrument	Date	Description
General Privacy Concern Index of Westin	1990	Four questions were used to divide consumers into three categories: high (fundamentalists), moderate (pragmatic) and low privacy concern (unconcerned) [19]
Consumer Privacy Concern Index of Westin	1991	Westin added two more business focus questions for the use of personal information to divide consumers into the three categories [19]
Medical Privacy Concern Index of Westin	1993	Westin added two medical concern questions to the Medical Sensitivity Index. Consumers were grouped in a high, medium or low privacy concern group [19]
Computer Fear Index of Westin	1993	Westin used three computer fear questions to create the index whereby the consumers were divided in three groups, namely high, medium and low computer privacy fear [19]
Distrust Index of Westin	1994	This index used four questions focusing on technology, government and business trust to identify a correlation between distrust and privacy issues. [19]
Privacy Concern Index of Westin	1996	The index used six questions to divide consumers in the privacy fundamentalists, privacy pragmatics and privacy unconcerned groups [19]
Concern for Information Privacy (CFIP)	1996	Develop the CFIP comprising four dimensions of privacy concerns, namely: collection, errors, unauthorized secondary use and improper access comprising 15 questions [1]
Privacy Segmentation Index Core Privacy Orientation Index	1995–1999	The privacy segmentation and core privacy orientation survey incorporated three questions focusing on a business context as well as whether existing laws and organizational practice provide privacy protection [19]
Concern for Information Privacy (CFIP)	2002	Stewart and Segars [7] used the CFIP of Smith et al. [1] containing 15 items in four dimensions, namely: collection, unauthorized secondary use, improper access and errors, adding computer anxiety and behavioral intention

(continued)

Table 1. (*continued*)

Instrument	Date	Description
Internet Users' Information Privacy Concern (IUIPC)	2004	Malhotra, Kim and Agarwal used the CFIP of Smith et al. [1], added the concepts of trust, behavioral intention and risk beliefs to measure the privacy concern of internet users [2]
Personal Internet Interest	2006	The authors used a personal internet interest variable with three questions focusing on privacy concern in the context of obtaining a service of information from the internet [20]
Information Privacy Concern about Peer Disclosure (IPCPD)	2015	Using the context of CFIP in an experiment with scenarios to identify privacy concern in social networking [21]
Social Media Users' Concern for Information Privacy	2015	The constructs of Stewart and Segars [7] and Malhotra et al. [2] were used to develop and validate social media users' concern for information privacy (CFSMIP) [22]
Information Privacy Concern towards Hospital Websites	2015	Three items from Bansal et al. (2010) [23] with items from Wu et al. [24] focusing on online privacy policy, reputation, information privacy concern, and behavioral intention [25]
CFIP, Willingness to Provide Personal Information (WPI)	2016	Adapting statements from Okazaki, Li and Hirose (2009) [26] and Malhotra et al. [2]. The constructs included CFIP, WPI, confidence in privacy protection (CPP), and perceived risk [26] with a total of 24 statements [27]
Internet Users' Information Privacy Concerns (IUIPC) & Personality Traits	2018	Researchers used the internet users' information privacy concerns (IUIPC) scale [2] together with scenarios to establish the relationship between IPC, recommendation accuracy and personality traits [10]
Information Privacy Concern during Social Website Interactions	2018	Twenty-two questions measuring the concern when disclosing personal information on websites. The questions were adapted from the work of Li [28] and Pavlou [29], among others [30]

(*continued*)

Table 1. (*continued*)

Instrument	Date	Description
Users' Information Privacy Concerns (UIPC)	2018	Users' information privacy concerns (UIPC) on privacy protection behavior (PPB) in social networks. The questionnaire included adapted statements from Dinev and Hart [31, 32]
Online Shopping Information Privacy Concern (IPC)	2019	Looking at information privacy concerns of online shopping consumers. One of the constructs was based on the information privacy concern construct of Pavlou [9, 29]
Demographic Characteristics & Information Privacy Concern (IPC)	2019	Researchers used the 16 items of Buchanan, Paine and Reips [33] to design a six-item survey focusing on the concern of sharing personal information over the internet in order to identify demographic differences [34]
CIFP in Health Information Exchange	2019	Using the CIFP of Stewart and Segars [7] and adapting it for health information exchange with opt-in intentions [35]
Mobile Users' Information Privacy Concerns (MUIPC)	2020	Mobile users' information privacy concerns (MUIPC) in the context of the internet of things, adapting survey items from Xu et al. [37], Solove [38] and Smit et al. [1, 39]
Mobile Users' Information Privacy Concerns (MUIPC)	2020	Using the antecedent-privacy-control-outcome model, adding computer anxiety, perceived control and app permission concerns for mobile users and adapting the work of Smith et al. [1], Malthota et al. [2], Stewart and Segars [7], Xu et al. [37] and Dinev, et al. [3, 40]

that the privacy experience of consumers influences their privacy concern together with other constructs such as gender, awareness of privacy policies, cultural differences [16] and age [34]. While the instruments aim to specifically measure concern for information privacy, they include statements that cover both users' concern and experience when their personal information is processed.

The "General Privacy Concern Index" of Westin is used to divide consumers into categories of concern; however, only one question concentrates on the concept of concern (namely, whether they are concerned about threats to their personal privacy) [2]. The other three questions focus on whether consumers agree on aspects relating to what business or government does in relation to privacy concepts based on their experience. The Consumer Privacy Concern Index included a question about the protection of privacy rights and if consumers agreed or disagreed with the statement, not necessarily measuring a concern. The questions used by Smith et al. [1:170] included concern questions such as "I'm concerned that companies are collecting too much personal information about me"; whereas other questions are phrased from an expectations perspective, such as "Companies should not use personal information for any purpose unless it has been authorized by the individuals who provided the information" [1:170]. Malhotra et al. [2] included questions from various authors with a concern, expectation or confidence perspective. A consumer concern question used is, for example, "I am concerned about threats to my personal privacy today" [2:352]. They also included questions from an expectations perspective, such as "Online companies should never sell the personal information in their computer datasets to other companies" [2:352]. Some questions are phrased from a confidence perspective, thus establishing if companies indeed exhibit certain values or behavior, for example: "Online companies are always honest with customers when it comes to using (the information) that I would provide" [2:352].

The CIFP or IUIPC were used in various studies to design new instruments to measure concern for information privacy in the context of each study, such as social networking [22, 32], online shopping [9] or mobile phones [3]. Others designed new instruments focusing on social networking and trust [41] and consumers' concerns in providing personal information for marketing purposes [42]. Researchers like Miyazaki and Fernandez [43] studied concern for information privacy from a risk perspective in terms of online shopping, finding that the more internet experience users have, the less privacy risk they perceive in terms of online shopping and security. Of importance to note is that Norberg et al. [44] studied the concept of the "privacy paradox" (a discrepancy between privacy attitude and privacy behavior as well as between privacy behavior and privacy intention). In their study, they found that the privacy paradox exists, whereby individuals disclose significantly more information than what they intent to disclose and behavior intent is not a predictor of actual behavior in a privacy context. Kokolakis [45] analyzed studies on the privacy paradox, supporting and challenging it. Each of these studies used a survey or experiment method to identify the dichotomy between privacy concern and behavior.

The studies discussed used various instruments for the concern of information privacy. These instruments include items that concentrate on the consumer's information privacy concern and/or expectations and/or experience in practice within a certain context. However, there is no balance of these items in that for each information privacy concern item, there is a corresponding expectation or experience statement to measure both perspectives. The instruments are also not aligned with best practice data privacy principles, such as the Fair Information Practice Principles (FIPPS) to measure information privacy concern and expectations in line with legal requirements with which organizations must comply.

The Online Information Privacy Culture Index (OIPCI) [15], used in this study, and the Information Privacy Culture Index (IPCI) [46, 47] consider both perspectives and expand on the concept of information privacy concern to also incorporate the privacy expectations and experience of data subjects as well as the concept of compliance with legal requirements. These questionnaires were developed in previous studies and measure for each FIPPs the expectation of the consumer together with their experience in practice as to whether it is met (thus their confidence that organizations are meeting that principle in practice). A number of specific concerns for information privacy statements are also included, making it comprehensive in terms of understanding the gap between information privacy expectations and experience, which outlines the concern for information privacy. The questions in the OIPCI and IPCI (as with the CIFP, UIPC, IUIPC and MUIPC) focus on concern for information privacy with statements from an expectation and experience perspective. The IPCI and OIPCI also measure the information privacy concern and gives an indication of the culture of privacy. In the context of this study, the instrument [15] is referred to as the Online Information Privacy Concern Instrument (OIPCI).

4 Methodology

This research employs a quantitative research design using a survey method. Surveys are useful to measure concern for information privacy; however, as a limitation it was found to be unreliable in terms of self-reporting of privacy behavior [45]. Privacy behavior is not measured in this study, only perceptions and attitudes.

4.1 Measuring Instrument

The OIPCI comprises 11 privacy principles, namely: accountability (AC), openness (OP), processing (use limitation) (PR), collection limitation (CL), purpose specification (PS), data subject participation (access) (DS), security safeguards (SS) and information quality (IQ), unsolicited marketing (UM), cross-border transfers (CB) and sensitive (special) personal information (SP). These were mapped to the POPI [15]. For each privacy principle, a question pair is used to measure the privacy expectation and experience (or confidence) of that principle being honored or implemented in practice by organizations. Information privacy concern can be identified where the expectation and experience about a specific principle do not match, thus where a gap is identified. The privacy principles map to the regulatory requirements of the POPI; therefore, if consumers experience that any of the requirements are not met in practice, it will also indicate a perception of non-compliance for organizations.

4.2 Sample

A thousand responses were collected in 2018 in South Africa, according to the demographic profile of the country. The sample included 52% males and 48% females. The age group of the sample were 16% between 18–24 years, 38% between 25 and 34 years, 39% between 35 and 54 years and 8% older than 55 years. The majority of the sample were employed (79%), with some participants unemployed (10%), students (8%) or retired (2.9%). Thirty percent of the participants had a school certificate and 3% had not completed school, 24% a diploma, 23% a university degree or diploma and 20% a postgraduate qualification. As stated, the participants represented the demographic profile of the country: 64% black, 20% white, 11% colored and 5% Indian. As such, the majority of the home languages spoken by the respondents were African languages.

The questionnaire was sent electronically by a market research company [48]. Ethical clearance was obtained from the university, ensuring that the survey met the ethical requirements such as being voluntary, anonymous and that consent was obtained to use the survey data for research publications.

5 Results

The respondents indicated that they obtained privacy information from the internet/websites (71%), banks (40%) and organizations to whom they provided their information (29%). The preferred methods to obtain privacy information, in order of preference, were: internet/websites, bank, government, organization to whom they provided their personal information and organizations they worked for. Sixty-three percent said that they knew of someone whose personal information had been misused (e.g. confidential information exposed), indicating that South Africans are experiencing data breaches. Ninety percent said that they were indeed concerned when providing their personal information on websites. They were mostly concerned about their identification (91%), financial (88%) and health (66%) information. Respondents were specifically concerned when websites built an online profile of them without consent (90%) or tracked their movements on the internet (82.8%).

The overall results showed that there was a gap in terms of the privacy expectations (4.43 mean) of respondents compared to the confidence (2.93 for mean) they had in whether organizations were meeting their expectations. Table 2 shows the means for each of the expectation and experience statements. All the expectation statements were significantly more positive compared with the corresponding experience statement based on the Sig. (two-tailed) test, which means that there was a significantly higher expectation for privacy than what consumers experienced in practice, thus their privacy expectations were not met. The three question pairs with the biggest discrepancy between expectation and experience were for the expectation that online companies would inform consumers if their personal data was lost, to only use their personal data for the agreed purposes and to protect their data when sending it to other countries. There was thus a significant gap in terms of the privacy expectations of consumers and what they experienced in practice, thus highlighting the concern for information privacy. If consumers feel that organizations are not meeting their privacy expectations, it also indicates that organizations might not be meeting regulatory requirements as the expectations statements are in line with the requirements of the POPI. This has an implication of non-compliance with legal requirements as well as a high concern for privacy amongst online consumers in SA.

Strategies can be implemented for meeting consumer expectations in order to address information privacy concern. Online organizations should understand their consumer base and if there are unique privacy concerns or expectations that they need to take cognizance of when designing websites, selling services or products online, conducting marketing and processing personal information. These could comprise an intervention for each of the IOPC item pairs with a gap to ensure that regulatory, process and technology controls are indeed in place. Furthermore, the privacy terms and conditions should be included clearly on online websites with additional communication and awareness.

Table 2. Means for privacy expectation and experience statements. (Items from [15])

Expectation statements, "I expect online companies (websites)…"	Mean	Experience/confidence statements, "I feel confident that online companies (websites) …"	Mean	Gap
16. "… to inform me if records of my personal data were lost damaged or exposed publically"	4.59	39. "… inform me if records of my personal data were lost damaged or exposed publically"	2.76	1.83
8. "… to only use my personal information for purposes I agreed to and never for other purposes than those agreed by me"	4.64	31. "I believe that online companies (websites) are only using my personal information for purposes I agreed to and never for other purposes"	2.84	1.8
22. "… to protect my information when they have to send it to other countries"	4.61	45. "… protect my information if they have to send it to other countries"	2.82	1.79
2. "… to use my personal information in a lawful manner"	4.62	25"… are using my personal information in lawful ways"	2.84	1.78
3. "I expect privacy when an online company (website) has to process my personal information for services or products"	4.59	26"… respect my right to privacy when collecting my personal information for services or products"	2.87	1.72
10. "… to obtain my consent if they want to use my personal information for purposes not agreed to with them"	4.59	33. "… are obtaining my consent to use my personal information for purposes other than those agreed to with me"	2.88	1.71
13. "… to protect my personal information"	4.56	36. "… are protecting my personal information"	2.86	1.70
7. "… to explicitly define the purpose for which they want to use my information"	4.59	30. "… are explicitly defining the purpose they want to use my information for"	2.92	1.67
5. "… to only collect my personal information when I have given my consent; or if it is necessary for a legitimate business reason"	4.58	28. "… are collecting my personal information only with my consent or for a legitimate business reason"	2.92	1.66
11. "… to inform me of the conditions for processing my personal information"	4.56	34. "… adequately inform me of the conditions for processing my personal information"	2.91	1.65
20. "… to honor my choice if I decide not to receive direct marketing"	4.58	43. "… honor my choice if I do not want to receive direct marketing"	2.94	1.64

(*continued*)

Table 2. (*continued*)

Expectation statements, "I expect online companies (websites)…"	Mean	Experience/confidence statements, "I feel confident that online companies (websites) …"	Mean	Gap
15. "… to ensure that their third parties (processing my personal information) have all the necessary technology and processes in place to protect my personal information"	4.51	38. "… ensure that their third parties have all the necessary technology and processes in place to protect my personal information"	2.90	1.61
14. "… to have all the necessary technology and processes in place to protect my personal information"	4.60	37. "… have all the necessary technology and processes in place to protect my personal information"	3.00	1.60
6. "… to only collect my personal information from myself and not from other sources"	4.49	29. "… are collecting my personal information from legitimate sources"	2.91	1.58
18. "… to correct or delete my personal information at my request"	4.56	41. "… will correct or delete my personal information at my request"	2.98	1.58
1. "… to notify me before they start collecting my personal information"	4.48	24. "… are notifying me before collecting my personal information"	2.92	1.56
17. "… to tell me what records of personal information they have about me when I enquire about it"	4.41	40. "… can tell me what records or personal information they have about me"	2.99	1.42
19. "… not to collect sensitive personal information about me"	4.31	42. "… only collect sensitive personal information about me with my explicit consent"	2.93	1.38
21. "… to give me a choice if I want to receive direct marketing from them"	4.51	44. Online companies (websites) always give me a choice to indicate if I want to receive direct marketing from them"	3.14	1.37
4. "… not to collect excessive or unnecessary information from me than what is needed for them to offer me a service or product"	4.35	27. "… are requesting only relevant and not information other than what is needed for them to offer me a service or product"	3.04	1.31
9. "… to only keep my personal information for as long as required for business purposes or regulatory requirements"	4.26	32. "I believe that online companies (websites) are keeping my personal information indefinitely"	3.26	1.00

(*continued*)

Table 2. (*continued*)

Expectation statements, "I expect online companies (websites)..."	Mean	Experience/confidence statements, "I feel confident that online companies (websites) ..."	Mean	Gap
12. "... to keep my personal information updated"	3.67	35. "... keep my personal information up to date"	2.95	0.72

It is recommended that online organizations conduct privacy compliance assessments to identify with which conditions of privacy legislation they do not comply in order to alleviate information privacy concern from that perspective.

5.1 Questionnaire Validation

Exploratory factor analysis was applied to the data using Principal Component Analysis as the extraction method. This was conducted separately for the expectations and experience factors. Varimax with Kaiser normalization was used as the rotation method, with three rotations. Two factors were identified for expectations and two for experience. Bartlett's test for sphericity and the Kaiser-Meyer Olkin (KMO) measure of sampling adequacy was found to be significant at $p < 0.00$, indicating validity of the sample where $p < 0.05$ [49]. Table 3 outlines the four factors with the corresponding items. Only item 23 was excluded, as it was an additional item which was added and can rather be interpreted as a yes/no question.

Table 3. Factors and Cronbach alpha.

Factor name	Items	Cronbach alpha	Total items
Factor A: Expectations	1, 2, 3, 4, 5, 6, 7, 8, 10, 11, 22	0.917	11
Factor B: Expectations	9, 12, 13, 14, 15, 16, 17, 18, 19, 20, 21	0.871	11
Factor C: Confidence	24, 25, 26, 27, 28, 29,30 31	0.958	8
Factor D: Confidence	32, 33, 34, 35, 36, 37, 38, 39, 40, 41, 42, 43, 44, 45, 46, 47	0.966	16

The KMO values were more than the minimum required 0.60 [50], namely 0.971 for expectations and 0.984 for confidence. Fifty-three percent of the variance was accounted for by the two expectations factors and 70% for the two experience factors, all with an Eigenvalue above one [51]. All the item values were above 0.4, which was the minimum for inclusion. The identified factors in this study closely resembles the factors of the first validation of the OIPCIQ study with 356 participants, where four factors were also identified [15]. Factor A includes the expectation statements relating to lawful processing, consent and collection. Similarly, factor C mostly includes the corresponding confidence statements about the same aspects. Factor B incorporates the expectation statements relating to the protection of the personal information such as security, third parties, direct marketing, and correction, whereas factor D also includes these statements from a confidence perspective.

As part of future research, further statistical analysis that investigates the correlation amongst the constructs and age groups will be conducted. A limitation of the this study is that a comparative analysis could not be conducted for the data collected in this study compared to the data collected in the first study [15]. The demographic profile of the first study was not representative of the South African population. Future research will aim to conduct a comparative study to monitor if there is a change in concern for information privacy over a period of time.

6   Conclusion

This paper outlines the concern for information privacy study which was conducted in South Africa. An overview of existing instruments was provided with a discussion of the OIPC instrument used in this study. The results indicated that while consumers have a high expectation for privacy, it is not met in practice by online organizations (websites). There is a large gap between what consumers expect in terms of privacy and how consumers perceive that online organizations are processing their personal information. While online organizations are not meeting consumer privacy expectations, they are also not meeting the minimum requirements of the POPI as perceived by consumers. The concern for information privacy is thus high in South Africa and corrective action is required from a government and online organization perspective. Further research should be aimed at extending the study to other jurisdictions for comparative results between countries for information privacy concern monitor the concern for information privacy over a period of time.

Acknowledgements. Women in Research Grant of UNISA.

References

1. Smith, H.J., Milberg, S.J., Burke, S.J.: Information privacy: measuring individuals' concerns about organizational practices. MIS Q. **20**(2), 167–195 (1996). https://doi.org/10.2307/249477
2. Malhotra, N.K., Kim, S.S., Agarwal, J.: Internet users' information privacy concerns (IUIPC): the construct, the scale and a casual model. Inf. Syst. Res. **15**(4), 336–355 (2014). https://doi.org/10.1287/isre.l040.0032
3. Degirmenci, K.: Mobile users' information privacy concerns and the role of app permission requests. Int. J. Inf. Manag. **50**(2020), 261–272 (2020). https://doi.org/10.1016/j.ijinfomgt.2019.05.010
4. RSA Data Privacy and Security Survey 2019: The growing data disconnect between consumers and businesses (2019). https://www.rsa.com/content/dam/en/misc/rsa-data-privacy-and-security-survey-2019.pdf

5. Varonis. 7 Must-know data breach statistics for 2020 (2020). https://www.varonis.com/blog/data-breach-statistics/
6. Palos-Sanchez, P., Saura, J.R., Martin-Velicia, F.: A study of the effects of programmatic advertising on users' concerns about privacy overtime. J. Bus. Res. **96**(2019), 61–72 (2019). https://doi.org/10.1016/j.jbusres.2018.10.0597
7. Stewart, K.A., Segars, A.H.: Examination empirical for information privacy of the concern instrument. Inf. Syst. Res. **13**(1), 36–49 (2002)
8. Xu, Z.: An empirical study of patients' privacy concerns for health informatics as a service. Technol. Forecast. Soc. Change **143**(2019), 297–306 (2019). https://doi.org/10.1016/j.techfore.2019.01.018
9. Li, Y., Liu, H., Lee, M., Huang, Q.: Information privacy concern and deception in online retailing: The moderating effect of online–offline information integration. Internet Res. **30**(2), 511–537 (2019). https://doi.org/10.1108/intr-02-2018-0066
10. Rook, L., Sabic, A., Zanker, M.: Engagement in proactive recommendations. J. Intell. Inf. Syst. **54**(1), 79–100 (2018). https://doi.org/10.1007/s10844-018-0529-0
11. Pentin, I., Zhang, L., Bata, H., Chen, Y.: Exploring privacy paradox in information-sensitive mobile app adoption: a cross-cultural comparison. Comput. Hum. Behav. **65**(2016), 409–419 (2016). https://doi.org/10.1016/j.chb.2016.09.005
12. Da Veiga, A.: The influence of information security policies on information security culture: illustrated through a case study. In: Furnell, S., Clarke N. (eds.) Proceedings of the Ninth International Symposium on Human Aspects of Information Security & Assurance (HAISA 2015), Lesvos, Greece, pp. 22–33 (2015)
13. Parliament of the Republic of South Africa. Protection of Personal Information Act (POPI) 4 of 2013, Cape Town (2013)
14. Botha, J., Eloff, M., Swart, I.: The effects of the POPI on small and medium enterprises in South Africa. In: Venter, H.S., Loock, M., Coetzee, M., Eloff, M.M, Flowerday, S. (eds.) Proceedings of the International Information Security South Africa (ISSA) Conference, Johannesburg, South Africa, pp. 1–8 (2015)
15. Da Veiga, A.: An online information privacy culture. In: Millham, R. (ed.) Proceedings of the Conference on Information Communications Technology and Society (ICTAS), Durban, South Africa, pp. 1–6 (2018)
16. Smith, H.J., Dinev, T., Xu, H.: Information privacy research: an interdisciplinary review. MIS Q. **35**(4), 989–1015 (2011)
17. Gavison, R.: Privacy and the limits of law. Yale Law J. **89**(3), 421–471 (1980). https://doi.org/10.2307/795891
18. Chellappa, R.K., Sin, R.G.: Personalization versus privacy: an empirical examination of the online consumer's dilemma. Inf. Technol. Manag. **6**, 181–202 (2005). https://doi.org/10.3138/cras.42.1.7
19. Kumaraguru, P., Cranor, L.F.: Privacy indexes: a survey of Westin's studies, CMU-ISRI-5-138, Institute for Software Research International School of Computer Science, Carnegie Mellon University, pp. 1–22 (2005)
20. Dinev, T., Hart, P.: An extended privacy calculus model for e-commerce transactions. Inf. Syst. Res. **17**(1), 61–80 (2006)
21. Chen, J., Ping, J.W., Xu, Y.C., Tan, B.C.Y.: Information privacy concern about peer disclosure in online social networks. IEEE Trans. Eng. Manag. **62**(3), 311–324 (2015). https://doi.org/10.1109/tem.2015.2432117
22. Osatuyi, B.: Is lurking an anxiety-masking strategy on social media sites? The effects of lurking and computer anxiety on explaining information privacy concern on social media platforms. Comput. Hum. Behav. **49**(2015), 324–332 (2015). https://doi.org/10.1016/j.chb.2015.02.062

23. Bansal, G., Zahedi, F.M., Gefen, D.: The impact of personal dispositions on information sensitivity, privacy concern and trust in disclosing health information online. Decis. Support Syst. **49**(2), 138–150 (2010)
24. Wu, K.W., Huang, S.Y., Yen, D.C., Popova, I.: The effect of online privacy policy on consumer privacy concern and trust. Comput. Hum. Behav. **28**(3), 889–897 (2012)
25. Kuo, K.M., Talley, P.C., Ma, C.C.: A structural model of information privacy concerns toward hospital websites. Program **49**(3), 305–324 (2015). https://doi.org/10.1108/prog-02-2014-0014
26. Okazaki, S., Li, H., Hirose, M.: Consumer privacy concerns and preference for degree of regulatory control. J. Advert. **38**(4), 63–77 (2009)
27. Anic, I.D., Budak, J., Rajh, E.: New information economy in post-transition countries: an economic approach to privacy concern. Transform. Bus. Econ. **15**(2), 165–178 (2016)
28. Li, Y.: The impact of disposition to privacy, website reputation and website familiarity on information privacy concerns. Decis. Support Syst. **57**(1), 343–354 (2014)
29. Pavlou, P.A., Liang, H., Xue, Y.: Understanding and mitigating uncertainty in online exchange relationships: a principal–agent perspective. MIS Q. **31**(1), 105–136 (2007)
30. Kaushik, K., Kumar, J.N., Kumar, S.A.: Antecedents and outcomes of information privacy concerns: role of subjective norm and social presence. Electron. Commer. Res. Appl. **32**(2018), 57–68 (2018). https://doi.org/10.1016/j.elerap.2018.11.003
31. Dinev, T., Hart, P.: Internet privacy concerns and their antecedents: measurement validity and a regression model. Behav. Inf. Technol. **23**(6), 413–422 (2004). https://doi.org/10.1080/01449290410001715723
32. Adhikari, K., Panda, R.K.: Users' information privacy concerns and privacy protection behaviors in social networks. J. Glob. Mark. **31**(2), 96–110 (2018). https://doi.org/10.1080/08911762.2017.1412552
33. Buchanan, T., Paine, C., Joinson, A.N., Reips, U.D.: Development of measures of online privacy concern and protection for use on the internet. J. Am. Soc. Inf. Sci. Technol. **58**(2), 157–165 (2007). https://doi.org/10.1002/asi.20459
34. Lee, H., Wong, S.F., Oh, J., Chang, Y.: Information privacy concerns and demographic characteristics: data from a Korean media panel survey. Gov. Inf. Q. **36**(2), 294–303 (2019). https://doi.org/10.1016/j.giq.2019.01.002
35. Esmaeilzadeh, P.: The effects of public concern for information privacy on the adoption of health information exchanges (HIEs) by healthcare entities. Health Commun. **34**(10), 1202–1211 (2019). https://doi.org/10.1080/10410236.2018.1471336
36. Xu, H., Teo, H., Tan, B.C., Argarwal, R.: Privacy concerns: a study of location-based services effects of individual self-protection, industry self-regulation, and government regulation on privacy concerns: a study of location-based services. Inf. Syst. Res. **23**, 1342–1363 (2012). https://doi.org/10.1287/isre.1120.0416
37. Xu, H., Teo, H., Tan, B.C.Y., Agarwal, R.: Effects of individual self-protection, industry self-regulation, and government regulation on privacy concerns: a study of location-based services. Inf. Syst. Res. **23**(4), 1342–1363 (2012). https://doi.org/10.1287/isre.1120.0416
38. Solove, D.J.: A taxonomy of privacy. Univ. PA Law Rev. **154**(3), 477–560 (2006). https://doi.org/10.2307/40041279
39. Foltz, C.B., Foltz, L.: Mobile users' information privacy concerns instrument and IoT. Inf Comput Secur. **28**(3), 359–371 (2020). https://doi.org/10.1108/ics-07-2019-0090
40. Dinev, T., Xu, H., Smith, J.H., Hart, P.: Information privacy and correlates: an empirical attempt to bridge and distinguish privacy-related concepts. Eur. J. Inf. Syst. **22**(2013), 295–316 (2013). https://doi.org/10.1057/ejis.2012.23
41. Dwyer, C., Hiltz, S., Passerini, K.: Trust and privacy concern within social networking sites: a comparison of Facebook and MySpace. In: Anderson, B.B., Thatcher, J., Meservy, R.D.,

Chudoba, K., Fadel, K.J., Brown, S. (eds.) Proceedings of the Thirteenth Americas Conference on Information Systems, Colorado, USA, pp. 1–13 (2007)

42. Phelps, J., Nowak, G., Ferrell, E.: Privacy concerns and consumer willingness to provide personal information. J. Public Policy Mark. **19**(1), 27–41 (2000)

43. Miyazaki, A.D., Fernandez, A.: Consumer perceptions of privacy and security risks for online shopping. J. Consum. Aff. **35**(1), 27–44 (2005). https://doi.org/10.1111/j.1745-6606.2001.tb0 0101.x

44. Norberg, P.A., Horne, D.R., Horne, D.A.: The privacy paradox: personal information disclosure intentions versus behaviors. J. Consum. Aff. **41**(1), 100–126 (2007). https://doi.org/10.1111/j.1745-6606.2006.00070.x

45. Kokolakis, S.: Privacy attitudes and privacy behaviour: a review of current research on the privacy paradox phenomenon. Comput. Secur. **64**(2017), 122–134 (2017). https://doi.org/10.1016/j.cose.2015.07.002

46. Da Veiga, A.: An information privacy culture index framework and instrument to measure privacy perceptions across nations: results of an empirical study. In: Furnell, S., Clark, S. (eds.) Proceedings of the Eleventh International Symposium on Human Aspects of Information Security & Assurance (HAISA), Adelaide, Australia, pp. 196–209 (2017)

47. Da Veiga, A.: An information privacy culture instrument to measure consumer privacy expectations and confidence. Inf. Comput. Secur. **26**(2018), 339–364 (2018)

48. InSites Consulting South Africa. https://insites-consulting.com/

49. Bartlett, J.E., Kotrlik, W.J., Higgins, C.C.: Organizational research: determining appropriate sample size in survey research. Inf. Tech. Learn. Perform. J. **19**(1), 43–50 (2001)

50. Kaiser, H.F., Rice, J.: Little jiffy, mark IV. Educ. Psychol. Meas. **34**, 111–117 (1974)

51. Hair, J.F., Anderson, R.E., Babin, B.J., Black, W.: Multivariate data analysis: a global perspective, 7th edn. Pearson, Upper Saddle River (2010)

Security Education, Training, and Awareness: Incorporating a Social Marketing Approach for Behavioural Change

Moneer Alshaikh[1,2] ⓘ, Sean B. Maynard[2(✉)] ⓘ, and Atif Ahmad[2] ⓘ

[1] Department of Cybersecurity, College of Computer Science and Engineering,
The University of Jeddah, Jeddah, Saudi Arabia
[2] School of Computing and Information Systems, Melbourne School of Engineering,
The University of Melbourne, Melbourne, VIC 3010, Australia
sean.maynard@unimelb.edu.au

Abstract. Effective information security education, training, and awareness (SETA) is essential for protecting organisational information resources. Although many organisations invest significantly in SETA, incidents resulting from employee noncompliance are still increasing. We argue that this may indicate that current SETA programs are sub-optimal in improving security compliance behaviour among employees, as they lack sufficient grounding in theory. This study proposes a new process for SETA development based on the social marketing approach. The proposed process involves selecting specific behaviour, developing a deeper understanding of the target audience, and using theory-informed intervention strategies for changing behaviour. The SETA development process provides a sound basis for future empirical work that will include focus groups and action research.

Keywords: Information security education training and awareness ·
Behavioural information security · Behaviour change · Social marketing

1 Introduction

Despite organisations investing significantly on cyber security education training and awareness (SETA), they still face a challenge around employees' noncompliance with security directives. A major proportion of non-malicious cyber security breaches result from employee noncompliance with an organisational cyber security directives [1]. This may indicate that many current SETA programs are deficient.

Security researchers consistently argue that SETA programs are important in ensuring employees' compliance with security directives [2, 3]. However, there is little guidance for organisations on how to develop effective SETA programs. Organisations rely on "best practice" and industry guidelines to develop SETA programs, but these generally have no empirical evidence or insufficient theoretical grounding. As a result, organisations lack guidance on selecting training strategies that are effective in particular contexts

© Springer Nature Switzerland AG 2020
H. Venter et al. (Eds.): ISSA 2020, CCIS 1339, pp. 81–95, 2020.
https://doi.org/10.1007/978-3-030-66039-0_6

[4, 5]. It therefore remains unclear how organisations can develop SETA programs that are effective in improving employee compliance with security directives.

Although information security behavioural research makes recommendations for practice, there is currently no basis for developing a SETA program that will consistently yield intended behaviour-change outcomes [6]. Öğütçü, Testik and Chouseinoglou [6] suggests, this is because SETA programs are not informed by behavioural change theories. Such theories provide systematic guidelines to organisations on conducting in-depth analysis of the behaviours that they wish to change and selecting appropriate strategies to most likely achieve intended outcomes.

Therefore, we draw on knowledge from the public health domain on using a social marketing approach for changing behaviour [7] and adopt a social marketing planning process [7] to develop a systematic and theory-informed SETA development process. The study addresses the following research question:

RQ: How can organisations develop effective SETA programs that improve employees' compliance behaviour?

Our study is motivated by the need for a systematic, theory-informed development process for SETA programs. Alshaikh, Maynard, Ahmad and Chang [4] found that organisations are unable to determine how effective their SETA programs are in influencing their employees' behaviour and how much they should invest in SETA programs to achieve effective outcomes. The social marketing approach can address this issue by providing systematic guidance to organisations on developing effective SETA programs.

This paper continues with a background section discussing information security behavioural studies and their contribution to the development of SETA programs. It then presents the social marketing approach and describes a new SETA development process based on social marketing, illustrating it using a phishing example. Finally, the paper concludes with a discussion of the theoretical and practical implications of the proposed SETA development process and directions for future work.

2   Background

This section provides background in the area of SETA, focusing on practical contributions to the development of SETA programs. It then discusses the key concepts and principles of social marketing, which provides the theoretical framing for this research.

2.1   Security Education Training and Awareness

Information security education training and awareness (SETA) programs refer to organised activities for the raising of awareness and the training of an organisation's employees [8]. The aim of a SETA program is to change the behaviour of employees with regard to security and to encourage good security practices [2, 9].

An extensive body of literature is devoted to developing effective SETA programs and understanding the effect of these programs on changing employee behaviour. Karjalainen and Siponen [10] identified 32 IS security training approaches, most based on practice.

Only 12 studies applied any theory (these included: learning theories, social psychology theories and criminology theories).

There are many useful practical contributions from existing theory-based SETA approaches. One such approach was to develop a generalized and validated method for implementing an Information Security Awareness Campaign [11]. The authors used three metrics (Awareness Importance, Awareness Capability, and Awareness Risk (AR)) drawn from the Information Security Awareness Capability Model (ISACM) to evaluate information security awareness campaigns.

Table 1 provides examples of studies and their practical recommendations for the development of SETA. Examples of practical recommendations from theoretical-grounded studies include using past experiences and collaborative learning to achieve desired outcomes [10], employing a combination of SETA delivery methods that activate and motivate employees [11], integrating the SETA program with the normal business communication of the organisation [12], applying SETA to address the gap between knowledge of risks and the capability to mitigate them [12], and engaging stakeholders in managing SETA activities through providing feedback [13]. However, these recommendations are fragmented and do not build cumulatively to guide the development of SETA programs in organisations.

Table 1. Examples of theory-based SETA studies and their practical recommendations

Exemplar Studies	Theory	Recommendations for SETA Programs
Kajzer, D'Arcy, Crowell, Striegel and Van Bruggen [13]	Personality traits (Machiavellianism and social desirability)	SETA programs should consider the personality traits and thinking styles of users
Vance, Siponen and Pahnila [14]	Habit theory and Protection Motivation Theory	SETA should address employees' past and automatic behaviour to improve compliance
Al-Omari, El-Gayar and Deokar [15]	Theory of Planned Behaviour	Identifies factors that SETA approaches should emphasize to influence the users' perspectives and knowledge
Karjalainen and Siponen [10]	Theory of Three Levels of Thinking	SETA programs should use past experiences and collaborative learning to achieve desired outcomes

Several researchers that there is a need for a systematic approach to developing SETA programs [10, 16, 17]. We argue that the process for developing SETA programs requires a systematic approach with a strong rationale. Theory should be used to inform SETA program development as it can provide detailed guidance on the analysis of the behaviour requiring change, and the selection of appropriate strategies and techniques to achieve the desired outcomes.

Given the lack of systematic and theory-informed SETA development processes from the academic literature, organisations tend to base their SETA development on conceptual guidelines and standards that lack support from empirical data, are generic in nature and do not consider the organisational context [5]. Further, implementing SETA based on these guidelines does not guarantee SETA quality [5]. Consequently, SETA programs are often implemented ineffectively, with the intended outcomes not being achieved. Therefore, this paper draws on the social marketing approach to design systematic and theory-informed interventions. The next section will discuss the social marketing approach and its adoption to inform the design of SETA programs.

2.2   Theoretical Framing – Social Marketing Approach

The social marketing approach could be useful for addressing the gap in the information security domain relating to the need for a systematic and theory-informed SETA development process. Social marketing is defined as "The systematic application of marketing alongside other concepts and techniques to achieve specific behavioural goals for social good" [18, p. 11]. Social marketing is well-recognized as a discipline focusing on influencing behaviour [7, 19]. Social marketing techniques are used effectively in areas such as public health and environmental sustainability. The objective of social marketing is to influence behaviour. The approach draws on behaviour theories and methodologies to solve social issues.

There are eight key social marketing concepts and principles as discussed below [20]. Understanding these principles is important for ensuring a more consistent approach to the development and evaluation of a social marketing campaign [18, 21].

a) **Customer Orientation.** The target audience (customer/employee) is the main focus of social marketing. Considerable effort is devoted to developing a thorough and comprehensive understanding of the target audience with data from different sources being combined and utilized.

Traditionally, in organisations that develop SETA programs to fulfil compliance requirements, the focus is not on the employees but rather on the internal and/or external parties that are tasked with enforcing the implementation of information security standards and regulations [4, 22]. A SETA manager will provide managers, and auditors (internal and external) with statistics on the number of employees who have completed the training and how many times they have undertaken this type of training. However, there are several disadvantages of this type of SETA program that is not 'employee oriented', such as limited consideration for employees' learning style [4]. Therefore, developing a SETA program using the 'customer/employee orientation' principle would improve the quality of the program as it would be based on a deeper understanding of employees.

b) **Behaviour and Behavioural Goals.** The social marketing approach aims to influence specific behaviours rather than just knowledge and attitude. Therefore, developing a good understanding of current behaviour is a core concept, and is achieved by first analysing the target audience behaviour (problem behaviour and desired behaviour) and then setting actionable and measurable behavioural goals, with key indicators identified for the specific social issue being addressed.

Setting appropriate objectives and goals for a SETA program is very important and well recognized in the literature [9]. Almost all best practice standards and guidelines advise organisations to set goals for their SETA programs [2]. However, objectives are usually limited to knowledge objectives and do not extend to belief and behaviour objectives [23]. A SETA program that includes knowledge, beliefs and behaviour objectives is more likely to be effective in changing employees' behaviour.

c) **Theory Based.** To effectively influence the target audience, social marketing uses behavioural theories to understand behaviour and to inform and guide the selection of appropriate intervention strategies. Interventions that are informed by theory are more successful and lead to longer lasting changes [24]. Several behavioural theories, models and frameworks (e.g. diffusion of innovation theory, self-control theory, health belief model and stage of change model) are frequently used by social marketers [7]. The theories explain what influences behaviour and the models describe the process of behaviour change [25]. This principle in the social marketing approach is particularly useful for addressing the lack of theory-informed SETA.

d) **Insight.** The social marketing approach focuses on developing a deep understanding and insight into what is likely to motivate the audience in a given context [21]. After developing a comprehensive understanding of the audience, further investigation is conducted to identify the key factors that are relevant for positively influencing behaviour. Investigation of the target audience leads to 'actionable insights' that can address factors related to the barriers and enablers of the desired behaviour [21].

The social marketing insight principle is particularly useful for the development of SETA programs as it provides the basis for an in-depth analysis of behaviour beyond the traditional 'needs assessment process' that current SETA best practice guidelines offer [23]. In current practice, the needs assessment for SETA uses different inputs to identify the problems and issues employees need to be aware of and comply with; whereas, the deeper understanding and insight into the target audience provided by the insight principle can identify enablers and barriers to performing the desired behaviour [23].

e) **Exchange.** Exchange theory, which was originally used in commercial marketing, postulates that for exchange to take place, the target audience must perceive benefits that are equal to or greater than the perceived costs [7]. In the social marketing context, the target audience tends to change their behaviour if they perceive that the benefits from adopting the desired behaviour are equal to or greater that the effort involved in performing the new behaviour or giving up unwanted behaviour [7]. Therefore, a social marketing campaign must include a compelling 'exchange' offer, based on a thorough analysis of the perceived/actual costs versus the perceived/actual benefits from adopting the new behaviour [19]. It aims to maximize the benefits and minimize the costs. The organisation's SETA development team can apply the exchange theory to effectively persuade employees to adopt the desired security behaviour through showing the benefits of the changed behaviour.

f) **Competition.** The social marketing competition principle refers to developing a comprehensive understanding of all factors that compete for the audience's time, attention and inclination to adopt the desired behaviour [21]. These should be identified and addressed to minimize the impact of competition.

A challenge that organisations face when implementing SETA is competing for their employees' time and attention [23]. Employees must complete many training modules that are specific to their job and responsibilities (health, occupational safety, etc.) which has created a situation where there is competition for an employee's time and attention. Several authors [e.g., 4, 16] have suggested that an organisation should build alliances with other organisational functions with the aim of integrating SETA into other training programs to reduce the number of training courses and therefore reduce the competition for an employee's attention.

g) **Audience Segmentation.** Audience segmentation is important for developing intervention strategies that are tailored to effectively influence behaviour [19]. This approach avoids the use of a generalized 'one size fits all' approach by dividing the target audience into smaller groups or 'segments' that share common beliefs, attitudes and behaviours [21]. Segments are prioritized and selected based on clear criteria, such as size and readiness to change [7].

In the cyber security domain, the SETA literature reports that the audience can be divided into groups based on their job descriptions and required skills and knowledge [9]. While the concept of 'audience segmentation' for a SETA program is not new, previous studies found that existing SETA programs mainly provide computer-based training (CBT) to all employees without attending to the specific needs of different segments of employees and their susceptibility to cyber security risk [4]. Therefore, applying audience segmentation in SETA programs may improve their effectiveness in influencing behaviour.

h) **Method Mix.** The social marketing approach applies an appropriate mix of methods to achieve the goals of the campaign. While it is important to use mixed methods to avoid reliance on a single approach, it is also important to integrate the methods to achieve synergy and enhance the overall impact [26]. There are five intervention strategies that can be implemented: design (to alter the environment), inform (to communicate facts and attitudes), control (to regulate and enforce), educate (to enable and empower) and service (to provide support services) [18].

In the cyber security domain, many studies [e.g., 27] recommend the use of a combination of SETA delivery methods; however, recommendations are usually focused on raising awareness using multiple channels and not on the implementation of a mix of intervention strategies, which is a far broader requirement for successfully influencing the behaviour of the target audience.

2.3 Summary of Social Marketing and SETA

Table 2 maps the social marketing key concepts and principles to the gaps in the existing SETA approaches. The next section proposes a SETA development process based on these social marketing key concepts and principles.

Table 2. Social marketing key concepts mapped to gaps in current SETA

Key Social Marketing Concepts	Description	Relevant Gaps in Current SETA Approaches
a) Customer Orientation	The customer is the central focus. All interventions directly address customer's needs	Existing SETA programs mainly aim to fulfil compliance requirements not on addressing employees' needs
b) Behaviour and Behavioural Goals	The social marketing approach aims to influence specific behaviours not just knowledge and attitude	Objectives are often limited to knowledge objectives and exclude belief and behaviour objectives
c) Theory Based	Social marketing applies behavioural theories to understand behaviour and inform and guide the selection of appropriate intervention strategies	Lack of theory-informed SETA programs to guide selection of appropriate intervention strategies
d) Develop 'Insight'	Social marketing is driven by 'actionable insights' that provide practical guidance for the selection and development of interventions	Traditional 'needs assessments' in SETA programs are limited and do not develop a deeper understanding of the employees' knowledge and attitudes
e) Exchange	Social marketing aims to maximize the potential 'offer' of a behavioural intervention and its value to the audience while minimizing all the 'costs' of adopting, maintaining, or changing a behaviour	Current SETA programs do not have compelling offerings that persuade employees to change their behaviour
f) Competition	Social marketing uses the concept of 'competition' to examine all the factors that compete for people's time for and attention to adopting a desired behaviour	External and internal competing factors are usually not considered
g) Audience Segmentation	Social marketing uses a 'segmentation' approach that ensures interventions can be tailored to people's different needs	Existing SETA programs mainly provide computer-based training (CBT) to all employees without paying attention to the specific needs of different segments of employees

(*continued*)

Table 2. (*continued*)

Key Social Marketing Concepts	Description	Relevant Gaps in Current SETA Approaches
h) Method Mix	Social marketing applies an appropriate mix of methods to achieve the goals of the campaign	Existing SETA programs are focused on raising awareness using multiple channels and not on the implementation of mix intervention strategies

3   Proposed SETA Development Process

The previous section discussed the social marketing key concepts and how applying these could address gaps in the cyber security domain. This section proposes a development process for SETA programs that incorporates the key concepts of the social marketing approach. In Fig. 1, we present a ten step process for developing a strategic social marketing plan as detailed by Lee and Kotler [7].

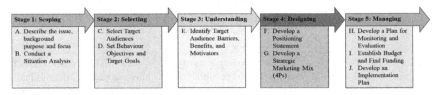

Fig. 1. The Proposed SETA Planning Process Adopted from Lee and Kotler [7]

The planning steps within Lee and Kotler [7]'s approach are spiral in nature (not linear), and provide a step-by-step approach providing a roadmap for the project. They suggest that it may be necessary to iterate through the model, i.e. refining the goals after gaining more understanding of the target audience or changing the communication channel based on the available budget. In the following sections, we discuss each phase.

3.1   Scoping Phase

The steps in the scoping phase (describe the issue, background purpose and focus, & conduct a situation analysis) aim to build foundational knowledge about the issues related to the area where social marketing campaigns are being designed.

A. **Describe the issue, background purpose and focus.** Data is gathered about the issue to which we are applying social marketing. To gather the data, a set of questions around the problem area needs to be developed and answered. This, in turn, allows the issue to be described in detail. Data may originate from scientific research, government, or organisational reports. Once enough data is collected, a statement of purpose is constructed that outlines the benefits of a successful campaign, as well as the primary focus of the campaign [7].

B. **Conduct a Situation Analysis.** An analysis of the external and internal factors that may have an effect on the campaign planning process is undertaken [7]. For instance, a SWOT (strength, weaknesses, opportunities, and threats) analysis may be undertaken that investigates the issue being addressed by the campaign within the organisation. This will result in a list of factors that guide the campaign planning process [7, 18].

3.2 Selecting Phase

There are 2 steps (select target audiences and set behaviour objectives and goals) within the Selecting Phase.

C. **Select Target Audiences.** In this phase we need to identify the group whose behaviour needs to be modified by the social marketing campaign [7]. A thorough description of the group (including the demographics, size, social network etc.) needs to be developed [7]. Different groups may be targeted by different campaigns designed to alter the same behaviour, so it is important to clearly define the target group. Lee and Kotler [7] suggest that this may involve segmenting the group population into several groups based on set criteria (e.g. problem incidence, problem severity, readiness & willingness to change, reach, and best match).

D. **Set Behaviour Objectives and Target Goals.** The specific objectives for the behaviour and the end goals of the campaign are designed based on the selected target audience group [7, 20]. This enables specific changes to behaviour to be targeted for each of the different groups identified. Three targets of behaviour have been described [7, 20]: raising awareness of the issues and create a need in the group to perform the desired behaviour (knowledge objectives); changing the target group's feelings and attitudes towards the issue (belief objectives); and changing the group's behaviour to either accepting, rejecting, modifying, abandoning, switching to, or continuing a target behaviour (behaviour objectives). Lee and Kotler [7] suggest that the goals of the behaviour change need to be specific, measurable, achievable, relevant, and timely so that the desired behaviour change can be quantified.

3.3 Understanding Phase

To understand the issues more thoroughly, additional understanding about the target audience and the desired behaviour is required by identifying target audience barriers, benefits, and motivators.

E. **Identify Target Audience Barriers, Benefits, and Motivators.** A thorough analysis is conducted in this step to understand the groups knowledge and attitudes towards the target behaviour and to identify any barriers that they face in order to adopt the desired behaviour [7, 21]. Additionally, the analysis will identify any benefits the group may have as a result of adopting the desired behaviour, as well as identifying the strategies to motivate the adoption of the desired behaviour, as well as whether there are individuals or other groups that can influence the group to adopt the desired behaviour. In conducting the behavioural analysis, data will be collected from multiple sources using a variety of data collection techniques (e.g. literature reviews, interviews, focus groups, direct observation and questionnaires) [7, 21]. Specific questions should be developed to identify barriers, benefits, and motivators.

3.4 Designing Phase

In the designing phase a positioning statement and strategic marketing mix are developed.

F. **Develop a Positioning Statement.** The positioning statement guides the development of the marketing mix and describes how the social marketing team wants the target group to see the desired behaviour [7, 28]. This is informed by on the Understanding Phase. The positioning statement includes strategies for dealing with behaviour, barriers, benefits or competition, depending on the behaviour change requirements [7].

G. **Develop a Strategic Marketing Mix (4Ps).** The traditional marketing 4P's (product, price, place and promotional strategies) are used as intervention tools to influence the target audiences' behaviour adoption [7]. From a product perspective, three types of products exist – core, actual and augmented. The core product represents the benefits that the group receives from adopting the correct behaviour. The actual product is the features of the desired behaviour and the resources supporting the desired behaviour. The augmented product is additional services that are promoted to the target audience. From the price perspective, this is where any costs for the target audience are identified along with any benefits they receive (these may be financial or non-financial). The place describes the location and timing where the targeted behaviour is performed. Promotion describes the communication strategies that will be utilized in four areas: the key message, the messengers, the communication channel, and the creative elements of the communication (e.g. logo, tags, graphics). The plan for promoting the need for the behaviour change is an integral aspect to ensure that the target audience knows about the product, price, and place, and that they can see the benefits of performing the desired behaviour.

3.5 Managing Phase

The managing phase develops a plan for monitoring and evaluation, establishes a budget and finds funding sources, and develops an implementation plan.

H. **Develop a Plan for Monitoring and Evaluation.** The success of the campaign will need to be assessed using four types of measures: input measures around the resources used in the campaign; output measures around the campaign activities; outcome measures focusing on target audience responses and changes in knowledge, beliefs and behaviour; and impact measures that assess the contribution to the effort's purpose [7]. The plan for monitoring and evaluation will state what measures are being used, how they will be used, and when they will be used [7]. It is recommended that the evaluation plan be developed before the budget is established to ensure this step is considered when it comes to determining the availability of resources.

I. **Establish Budget and Find Funding Sources Budget.** In this step the resources required for the social marketing plan are identified and any funding required (or sources for funding) is determined [7]. At this stage of the process, a revision of previous steps may be trigged if the resource availability limits the social marketing program in any way [7]. Also, the budget for the social marketing program is presented here.

J. **Develop an Implementation Plan.** The implementation plan within social marketing replicates a "real" marketing plan as it defines the roles and responsibilities, tasks, and schedule of the campaign activities [7]. The plan is shared between relevant stakeholders to inform them of the behaviour change activity taking place. Lee and Kotler [7] suggest that sustainable behaviour change can only be achieved if the implementation plan details a plan to maintain the behaviour change in the long term.

4 Application of the Proposed SETA Planning Process

A significant challenge for any organisation is employee non-compliant security related behaviour [1]. Many cyber-breaches have exploited vulnerabilities involving human behaviour, such as clicking on phishing emails or disclosing passwords [29]. The proposed SETA development process can assist organisations in altering human security related behaviours by: 1) providing a systematic planning process that integrates social marketing principles to successfully influence behaviour, 2) developing a thorough, in depth understanding of the target audience to guide the development of effective SETA, and 3) applying various interventions to influence behaviour.

Our proposed social marketing enabled SETA development process aims to specifically address particular security related employee behaviours. These behaviours might, for example, include behaviour related to knowledge leakage, protecting credentials (e.g., passwords), or improving employees' responses to phishing emails. Table 3 presents an illustration of the proposed SETA development process using the example of behaviour related to phishing given the considerable challenge that phishing represents for many organisations [1].

The phishing example shows that the proposed SETA development process can be applied to address issues related to employee's behaviour within the cybersecurity context. Furthermore, the example can guide organisations on how the proposed SETA development process should be used to improve the effectiveness of SETA program.

Table 3. The proposed SETA development process illustrated using a phishing example

---

Phase 1: Scoping

A) Describe the issue, background purpose and focus: a statement about the prevalence of the issue (e.g. more than half of the security incidents are related to employees clicking on unsafe links), a statement of the financial or reputational cost to the organisation (e.g. the or-ganisation has lost $x as a result of these incidents), a statement on the purpose of the cam-paign (e.g. to address phishing attacks by improving employee responses to phishing emails)

B) Conduct a Situation Analysis: Using a SWOT analysis on the phishing issue may give the following results:

Strengths: high level of awareness top management around cyber-threats, awareness that phishing is a major threat

Weaknesses: limited resources available for the campaign (e.g. staff, budget)

Opportunities: able to align the campaign with other cyber security activities (international cyber security day, safer internet day, stay smart online etc.); ability to utilize resources from external bodies such as government, or consultants (e.g. templates, or using popular social media hashtags etc.) to enhance the message

Threats: increasing level of sophistication of phishing emails (e.g. using foreign characters in addresses that are hard to distinguish from the original - http://www.microsoft.com/- note the small Cyrillic barred 'o')

Phase 2: Selecting

C) Select Target Audiences: Groups within the organisation will be segmented based on their roles and responsibilities, departments, and level. Each group segment should be evaluated based on size, ability to reach and susceptibility to phishing attacks

D) Set Behaviour Objectives and Target Goals: The main target goal for phishing behaviour change is to protect the organisation from phishing by reducing employee propensity to click and increasing their propensity. We can measure the success of the campaign though assessing if there are less incidents caused by phishing, and whether more phishing attacks are reported

---

Phase 3: Understanding

E) Identify Target Audience Barriers, Benefits, and Motivators: A set of focus groups be held with the target group to determine their existing knowledge about phishing attacks, the barriers preventing them from identifying phishing emails, and the motivators for reporting phishing emails. Outcomes of the focus group might be that employees do not have enough knowledge to identify phishing links, may not have the time to spend reporting them, or find it inconvenient to do so

---

Phase 4: Design

F) Develop a Positioning Statement: we want employees to believe that clicking on phishing links has a detrimental effect on the organisation and that appropriately reporting phishing emails protects the organisation and others from harm

G) Develop a Strategic Marketing Mix (4Ps):

Product: a reporting mechanism, a checking mechanism, and a feedback mechanism back to employees to show that their reporting is valued

Price: employees showing irresponsible behaviour by repeatedly clicking on phishing links can affect the employee's employment (costing their jobs, or promotions)

Place: the organisational context

Promotion: email, internal social media, or physical training

---

(continued)

Table 3. (*continued*)

Phase 5: Managing
H) Develop a Plan for Monitoring and Evaluation: The <u>outcome measures</u>: a pre-measurement of the number of phishing reports prior to the campaign and then compare this to the number of phishing reports after the campaign. The <u>impact measure:</u> the decrease in phishing incidents has made a difference to the overall protection of the organisation's systems
I) Establish Budget and Find Funding Sources Budget: A budget would be prepared listing the costs associated with the phishing prevention campaign including the development of resources such as posters and training materials for phishing awareness, and for the development of evaluation exercises (e.g. phishing exercises)
J) Develop an Implementation Plan: A list of tasks needs to be developed, along with the specification of the roles and responsibilities of personnel. A specific timetable needs to be established in conjunction with the security team, trainers, and the identified behaviour change target group

5 Conclusion and Future Work

This paper presents a systematic and theory-informed development process for SETA programs based on the social marketing approach. The need for a systematic and theory-informed SETA development process is explained, and application of the social marketing approach and the social campaign planning process in the information security domain is discussed.

The main contribution of this research to theory is an explanation of how the social marketing approach can be applied in the information security domain, which addresses the gap in the literature for a systematic SETA development process. The social marketing approach presented in this paper and the related planning process can guide organisations in selecting a specific behaviour, identify the target audience, understand the barriers, benefits and motivators for performing the desired behaviour and then design a SETA program with mix intervention and marketing strategies to achieve behaviour change.

This study has several important implications for practice. The study has proposed a new process that can be used by organisations to develop an effective SETA program that can positively influence employees' behaviour. The study has also provided practical guidance to organisations on how to use social marketing to develop their SETA programs. The example of the problem of phishing attacks was used to demonstrate how the social marketing planning process can be applied in the cyber security domain.

The proposed SETA program based on the social marketing approach provides a sound basis for further research. The next step is to conduct a focus group with information security training and awareness managers/experts to validate and refine the proposed SETA development process and explore what the experts think about the practicality and utility of such an approach. The final step of the research project will be conducting an action research study by putting the proposed SETA development process into practice in an organisation with a high level of maturity in SETA practices. This research will be undertaken by selecting a specific behaviour and target audience, understanding the barriers, benefits and motivators of the target audience to perform the desired behaviour and then designing a SETA program with mix intervention strategies to influence the target audience behaviour. Further, the social marketing approach can be applied to other training fields, which gives researchers ample opportunity to test and to refine the approach through its application in various training domains.

References

1. NTT Security: Global Threat Intelligence Report. NTT Security (2019). https://www.nttsec urity.com/docs/librariesprovider3/resources/2019-gtir/2019_gtir_report_2019_uea_v2.pdf
2. Tsohou, A., Karyda, M., Kokolakis, S., Kiountouzis, E.: Managing the introduction of information security awareness programmes in organisations. Eur. J. Inf. Syst. **24**, 38–58 (2015)
3. Posey, C., Roberts, T.L., Lowry, P.B.: The impact of organizational commitment on insiders' motivation to protect organizational information assets. J. Manag. Inf. Syst. **32**, 179–214 (2015)
4. Alshaikh, M., Maynard, S.B., Ahmad, A., Chang, S.: An exploratory study of current information security training and awareness practices in organizations. In: Proceedings of the 51st Hawaii International Conference on System Sciences, pp. 5085–5094 (2018)
5. Siponen, M., Willison, R.: Information security management standards: problems and solutions. Inf. Manag. **46**, 267–270 (2009)
6. Öğütçü, G., Testik, Ö.M., Chouseinoglou, O.: Analysis of personal information security behavior and awareness. Comput. Secur. **56**, 83–93 (2016)
7. Lee, N.R., Kotler, P.: Social Marketing: Changing Behaviors for Good. Sage Publications, Thousand Oaks (2015)
8. D'Arcy, J., Hovav, A., Galletta, D.: User awareness of security countermeasures and its impact on information systems misuse: a deterrence approach. Inf. Syst. Res. **20**, 79–98 (2009)
9. Whitman, M.E., Mattord, H.J.: Management of Information Security. Thomson Course Technology, Boston (2008)
10. Karjalainen, M., Siponen, M.: Toward a new meta-theory for designing information systems (IS) security training approaches. J. Assoc. Inf. Syst. **12**, 518–555 (2011)
11. Scrimgeour, J.-M., Ophoff, J.: Lessons learned from an organizational information security awareness campaign. In: Drevin, L., Theocharidou, M. (eds.) WISE 2019. IAICT, vol. 557, pp. 129–142. Springer, Cham (2019). https://doi.org/10.1007/978-3-030-23451-5_10
12. Poepjes, R.: The development and evaluation of an information security awareness capability model: linking ISO/IEC 27002 controls with awareness importance, capability and risk. University of Southern Queensland (2015)
13. Kajzer, M., D'Arcy, J., Crowell, C.R., Striegel, A., Van Bruggen, D.: An exploratory investigation of message-person congruence in information security awareness campaigns. Comput. Secur. **43**, 64–76 (2014)
14. Vance, A., Siponen, M., Pahnila, S.: Motivating IS security compliance: insights from habit and protection motivation theory. Inf. Manag. **49**, 190–198 (2012)
15. Al-Omari, A., El-Gayar, O., Deokar, A.: Information security policy compliance: the role of information security awareness. In: Americas Conference on Information Systems (AMCIS) (2012)
16. Puhakainen, P., Siponen, M.: Improving employees' compliance through information systems security training: an action research study. MIS Q. **34**, 757–778 (2010)
17. Cram, W.A., D'arcy, J., Proudfoot, J.G.: Seeing the forest and the trees: a meta-analysis of the antecedents to information security policy compliance. MIS Q. **43**, 525–554 (2019)
18. French, J., Merritt, R., Reynolds, L.: Social Marketing Casebook. Sage, Thousand Oaks (2011)

19. McKenzie-Mohr, D.: Fostering Sustainable Behavior: An Introduction to Community-Based Social Marketing. New Society Publishers, Gabriola (2011)
20. French, J., Blair-Stevens, C.: Social Marketing Pocket Guide (2005)
21. French, J., Blair-Stevens, C., McVey, D., Merritt, R.: Social Marketing and Public Health: Theory and Practice. Oxford University Press, Oxford (2010)
22. Spitzner, L.: Defining the Security Awareness Maturity Model. Security Awareness, vol. 2019. SANS (2016)
23. Alshaikh, M., Naseer, H., Ahmad, A., Maynard, S.B.: Toward sustainable behaviour change: an approach for cyber security education training and awareness. In: European Conference on Information Systems, p. 15 (2019)
24. Michie, S., Atkins, L., West, R.: The Behavior Change Wheel: A Guide to Designing Interventions. Silverback Publishing, Great Britain (2014)
25. Glanz, K., Rimer, B.K.: Theory at a glance: a guide for health promotion practice. US Department of Health and Human Services, Public Health Service (1997)
26. Sowers, W., French, J., Blair-Stevens, C.: Lessons learned from social marketing models in the United Kingdom. Soc. Mark. Q. **13**, 58–62 (2007)
27. Abawajy, J.: User preference of cyber security awareness delivery methods. Behav. Inf. Technol. **33**, 237–248 (2014)
28. Grier, S., Bryant, C.A.: Social marketing in public health. Ann. Rev. Public Health **26**, 319–339 (2005)
29. Office of the Australian Information Commissioner: Notifiable Data Breaches Quarterly Statistics Report (2019). https://www.oaic.gov.au/privacy/notifiable-data-breaches/notifiable-data-breaches-statistics/

Exploring Emotion Detection as a Possible Aid in Speaker Authentication

Ebenhaeser Otto Janse van Rensburg$^{(\boxtimes)}$ ⓘ, Reinhardt A. Botha ⓘ,
and Rossouw Von Solms ⓘ

Nelson Mandela University, Eastern Cape, South Africa
{s213295245,ReinhardtA.Botha,Rossouw.VonSolms}@mandela.ac.za

Abstract. Voice as an authentication method is yet to be widely implemented as it is not yet as accurate as other authentication methods. In addition, it may be easy to coerce an authentic individual to authenticate themselves by means of voice. If an individual were authenticated under duress, the proper steps would need to be taken to mitigate any possible damage. Thus, this study attempted to verify the possibility of the addition of emotion detection as an aid in speaker authentication. Multiple experiments were conducted using two classifiers, namely a multilayer perceptron and a random forest. These experiments utilized different combinations of the mel-frequency cepstral coefficients, chroma, mel spectrogram, contrast, and tonnetz features. The experiments did not achieve the accuracy of other biometric authentication systems. However, they provided insight into the possible implementation of an emotion detection system and the value of each feature. Although the results from such a system may not be accurate enough to base an authentication decision on, additional security-related measures may be warranted if possible duress is detected.

Keywords: Speaker authentication · Emotion detection · RAVDESS · MLP · MFCC

1 Introduction

A common approach to securing information is requiring an individual to be authenticated before being granted access to it. However, there are multiple inherent flaws in traditional authentication methods. Recent developments have increased the possibility of biometrics being utilized as an authentication method, which could improve the ease of access to information and increase security in some instances. Facial recognition and fingerprint recognition, for example, are accurate enough to secure sensitive information on mobile devices. This paper will explore the potential and the utilization of voice as an authentication method. The adoption of voice as an authentication method could be instantaneous, as the hardware required to authenticate by means of voice, a microphone, is already present in most mobile devices. Other biometric authentication

© Springer Nature Switzerland AG 2020
H. Venter et al. (Eds.): ISSA 2020, CCIS 1339, pp. 96–111, 2020.
https://doi.org/10.1007/978-3-030-66039-0_7

methods may require special equipment that is not as readily available as microphones. However, accurate voice authentication can not determine whether an individual was authenticated under duress, nor can other non-biometric authentication methods. Therefor, this paper will also explore the potential of identifying emotion through voice to ultimately determine the feasibility of combining emotion detection with a speaker authentication system. Although two classifiers were tested, the point of the study was not to compare the two, but to explore the potential of emotion detection systems.

This paper starts by discussing authentication (Sect. 2). It hones in on biometric authentication with a focus on voice (Sect. 2.1) and its problems (Sect. 2.2). Thereafter, Sect. 3 discusses how emotion is portrayed through voice. Section 4 outlines feature extraction techniques and models that utilize voice. The experimental procedure (Sect. 5) is used to test two classifiers with a view of exploring the potential of an emotion detection system by utilizing multiple examples. This is followed by a discussion of the results (Sect. 6) before the paper concludes (Sect. 7).

2   Authentication

In the digital age, the majority of sensitive information is stored in digital form. In order to gain access to this sensitive information, individuals must first be authenticated by using at least one of the three factors of authentication, namely something you know, something you have, and something you are [2].

The first factor of authentication, something you know, requires the individual to provide information that only the authentic individual would possess, a secret. Within a traditional username and password combination, the secret would take the form of the password. Although it is ill-advised, individuals often write passwords down because they have difficulty remembering them, resulting in multiple security concerns [28, p. 14]. The second factor of authentication, something you have, takes the form of a physical token, for example a hotel room card. In order to gain access to the room, the individual first needs to present the card. Unfortunately, such cards are often lost or stolen and could possibly grant access to unauthorized individuals. The first and second factors of authentication are often combined to increase the level of security. For example, an individual may need to provide a bank card as well as a valid PIN in order to gain access to an ATM. The final factor of authentication, something you are, refers to human characteristics that cannot be lost, stolen, or forgotten easily.

Owing to this, using the final factor of authentication should be more secure than using the previous two. Authentication using the first and second factor of authentication provides definitive results, which are either positive or negative. However, the use of the third factor could produce non-definitive results. Although this factor needs to take into account the possibility of non-definitive results, authentication using human characteristics (biometrics) could improve current security measures.

2.1 Biometrics for Authentication

Biometric traits can be divided into two categories, namely behavioural traits and physiological traits [4]. Authenticating an individual by means of behavioural biometric traits, such as signatures, keystrokes, or voices, entails capturing and comparing them to previously captured data. These biometric traits enable the authentication of individuals without their knowledge, as unobtrusive techniques can be used to capture them. Additionally, some behavioural traits, such as keystroke dynamics, are often already being captured. In such cases, the only alteration needed may be the implementation of a system that analyzes the behaviour [7].

Considering that existing security measures result in absolute acceptance or rejection, while biometrics do not result in absolute outcomes, improving existing security measures by means of biometrics can prove difficult. When a facial recognition system attempts to calculate the distance between an individual's eyes, the image used may not always capture the exact distance between the eyes. For this reason, biometric system often results are often accepted as being 'close enough' when authenticating an individual. When testing and improving a biometric authentication system, failures result in either false positives or false negatives. The rejection of authentic individuals results in false negatives, whereas the acceptance of inauthentic individuals results in a false positives. The accuracy of the system is determined by adding up these results and comparing this number to the number of tests conducted, resulting in the Equal Error Rate (ERR).

Voice as a biometric authentication method is considered a behavioural biometric, and as such, it can be captured without the knowledge of the individual being authenticated. Additionally, it can be captured using existing tools, such as mobile phone microphones. This method of authentication also allows for the authentication of an individual in a different location, serving as a possible alternative to security questions for financial institutions. Unfortunately, authenticating individuals over the phone introduces multiple changing variables to the authentication system, most prominently the use of different types of microphones. These changing variables can be addressed through the approach taken to authentication by means of voice.

Text-Dependent vs Text-Independent Speaker Authentication. Two prominent approaches to voice-based biometric authentication exist, namely text-dependent and text-independent authentication [6,24,29]. Enrolling into a text-dependent speaker authentication system requires an individual to record themselves speaking a predefined sentence or phrase [6,16]. To be authenticated at a later stage, the same individual must speak the same predefined sentence. Provided that this authentication method is accurate, it could prove to be more secure than traditional authentication methods. However, it is still susceptible to pre-recorded audio samples.

Alternatively, a text-independent speaker authentication system allows an individual to enroll by recording any spoken sentence or phrase [6,29]. Later on the individual will be authenticated when they speak any sentence or phrase irrespective of what the recorded sentence or phrase was, provided that it is the authentic individual speaking. Although this authentication method may also be influenced by pre-recorded audio samples, additional steps can be taken to negate such attacks that are not viable when using a text-dependent approach. One such method entails requiring the individual to provide an answer to a math equation or security question. In such an case, authentication of the provided audio sample will be conducted only in the event that the security question is answered correctly. The freedom provided by this authentication method may make it difficult for it to achieve the same accuracy as text-dependent speaker authentication.

Text-Dependent Speaker Authentication Systems. Text-dependent speaker authentication is not widely implemented, as it has more disadvantages than other biometric authentication methods, such as fingerprint authentication [21]. Regardless, provided that speaker authentication matches the accuracy of fingerprint authentication, numerous systems could benefit from the implementation of this authentication method.

A large number of mobile phones allow individuals to instruct their devices to act on commands, provided that these are preceded by a predefined phrase, such as 'OK Google'. These devices already posses the ability to understand their users. They capture and store their users' voices, and their voice recognition improves through continuous use. However, any individual is able to instruct any device, regardless of whether own it.

In the event that any biometric authentication system became accurate enough to reject all fraudulent attempts at access, the only possible way for an inauthentic individual to gain access to the system would be to coerce the authentic individual into providing it.

2.2 Speaker Authentication Under Duress

Biometrics as an authentication method may be an improvement on traditional methods of authentication; however, the possibility of bypassing it through other techniques still exists. Some fingerprint authentication systems, for example, perform their authentications by comparing the distances between the ridges on fingers. Such physiological traits cannot be altered easily, and as such, the systems may not recognize small changes as concerning.

The combination of biometrics being a 'close enough' authentication method and behavioural traits requiring the constant accommodation of changing factors may lead to the development of a system that not only accurately authenticates an individual, but also detects whether the individual has been forced to be authenticated. Such a system will first authenticate the individual and then determine whether the authentication was performed under duress. Similar research has investigated the utilization of keystroke authentication to determine whether an individual was forced into being authenticated by identifying predefined inaccuracies. If this was found to be the case, corrective action could be taken [7]. In order to implement such an approach, a text-dependent speaker authentication system would first need to authentication an individual accurately through voice. A successful authentication would result in the system determining whether the individual performed this authentication under duress, through the use of emotion.

3 Emotion Through Voice

The two predominant theories of emotion classification are the discrete emotion theory and the dimensional theory [9]. The discrete emotion theory states that emotions consist of biological and neurological profiles. These profiles are, happy, anger, sad, fear, disgust, surprise, and neutral, known as 'Universal emotions' [9]. The dimensional theory states that emotion is portrayed through two identifiable characteristics, namely valence and arousal. The dimensional theory thus condenses all emotions into three categories, namely positive, neutral, and negative emotions [9].

The entire human body can contribute to the portrayal of an emotion, including a person's voice through the production of sound. The majority of this sound is produced by the larynx, also known as the voice box. The voice box, in combination with the lips, tongue, and jaw, contributes to speech.

A tutoring system may be positively impacted by the implementation of emotion detection. The tutoring system could decrease the speed of lessons when a negative emotion is detected. Students may not overtly convey any difficulties that they face with the material. Subsequently, these will not affect the rate of the provided lessons and will possibly worsen the students' understanding of future lessons.

4 Feature Extraction Techniques and Models

Features found within speech are separated into behavioural features and acoustic features. Behavioural features include the use of vocabulary, the flow of speech, and changes in pitch, among others. Acoustic features include F0 variability and voice intensity. F0, also known as the fundamental frequency, is the lowest frequency of a given waveform, measured in Hertz (Hz). Voice intensity refers to how loud a sound was produced, measured in decibels (dB).

4.1 Feature Extraction Techniques

The system created for this paper utilized multiple feature extraction techniques in order to attempt to improve upon the accuracy achieved by systems that utilize each technique independently. These feature extraction techniques were used to extract the mel-frequency cepstral coefficients (MFCC), chroma, mel spectrogram, contrast, and tonnetz. The MFCC extraction technique is used more frequently than the other techniques when extracting features from audio [25]. Each technique will now be expanded upon.

MFCC. The process of creating MFCC features starts with the framing and windowing of the audio signals [23]. As audio signals are always changing, capturing these signals at the correct intervals, or framing, will improve the results. Samples that are too small may provide too little data, and samples that are too large may include too many changing values [1]. These short frames often range from 10 to 50 millisecond frames. Further smoothing the edges of newly created frames is called windowing. Windowing is often performed by using the Hamming window [5]. The second step entails estimating the power spectrum of each frame. This step is often performed by making use of the discrete fourier transform (DFT). The third step applies the mel filter bank to the power spectrum to determine the amount of energy within various frequency groupings. The fourth step involves the extraction of the logarithm from the filter bank. The logarithm is calculated because it mimics what a human ear would hear, as the perceived energy is not necessarily the same as the produced energy [30]. The fifth, and final, step concludes the process by calculating the discrete cosine transform (DCT) of the logarithm filter banks [8]. As some filter banks overlap, they often correlate with one another. This final step decorrelates these filter bank energies, resulting in the possibility of modelling the features with, for example, a Gaussian mixture model.

Chroma. Chroma features relate to the 12 pitch classes within music and focus on the sound 'quality', or tone, also known as timbre. The 12 pitch classes correspond to an equal temperament scale that extracts the 12 values from an octave by dividing it into equal steps represented by C, C♯, D, D♯, E , F, F♯, G, G♯, A, A♯, and B [15]. Additionally, an octave can be considered as the interval between a musical pitch (C) and another pitch (C) with double the frequency. One chroma vector would thus represent the 12 pitch classes observed in Western music. However, additional chroma vectors could be utilized, provided that they were calculated using multiples of 12 [26]. There are multiple approaches to computing chroma features, one of which entails extracting 88 frequency bands that correspond to the musical notes ranging from A0 to C8, spanning over eight octaves [15,20]. Short-time metrics would then be calculated for each of the 88 subbands. These could include short-time root-mean squares (STRMSs) or short-time fourier transforms [19,20]. Finally, the energy distribution relative to the 12 pitch classes would be computed to create the chroma features.

The 12 pitch classes can be observed in Fig. 1.

Mel Spectrogram. An audio sample is often visualized as a two-dimensional image that can be created by making use of three values, namely the two acoustic features, Hz and dB, as well as Time (s). However, this two-dimensional image is not an accurate representation of the provided sound sample. A three-dimensional image, called a spectrogram, would better serve to portray the three values. An example of a spectrogram is shown in Fig. 2.

The mel spectrogram follows a similar process to the MFCC. An audio sample is firstly separated into windows, followed by the computation of the fast fourier

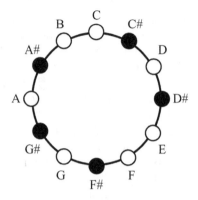

Fig. 1. Chroma circle

Fig. 2. Spectrogram

transform (FFT) of each window. A mel filter bank is generated by dividing the entire frequency spectrum into evenly spaced frequencies. The process concludes by determining the power of the signal throughout the various frequency groupings. This process does not compute the logarithm, nor does it apply the DCT, as these steps are used to create a sound similar to what a human would hear. A mel spectrogram simply applies a mel scale to a spectrogram.

Contrast. The spectral contrast follows a process more similar to that of the MFCC than that of the mel spectrogram. First, the FTT is computed to estimate the power spectrum. Therafter a mel filter bank is applied to determine the amount of energy within the various frequency groupings. The spectral contrast extracts the strengths of the peaks and valleys within each subband, as well as the differences between them, while the MFCC extracts only the sum of the strengths within each subbands [13,14]. Similarly to the MFCC, the spectral contrast calculates the logarithm of the strengths, followed by the DCT. Additionally, some systems make use of octave-based spectral contrast features. In these cases, the mel filter bank is replaced by an octave-scale filter and the DCT is replaced by a Karhunen-Loeve transform (KLT) [31].

Tonal Centroids. Tonal centroids, or tonnetz, sre lattice diagrams representing tonal relationships, they are also known as harmonic networks. An example of a tonnetz grid can be observed in Fig. 3 [12].

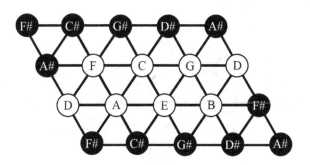

Fig. 3. Tonnetz

The tonal centroids are calculated by extracting the chroma features from an audio sample. These features are assigned values based on the tonnetz lattice diagram through the use of a harmonic change detection function (HCDF), or harmonic centroid transform, as shown in Fig. 3. The process is concluded by applying a selected smoothing filter before calculating the distances of the tonal relationships [10,12].

4.2   Models

The extracted features need to be categorized into groups reflecting the identified emotions. Two approaches to categorizing the features are classification and clustering. Classification groups data by utilizing already defined groups as well as predefined labels and supervised learning. Clustering groups data based on similarities through the use of unsupervised learning without predefined labels. This study utilized two classification techniques, namely multilayer perceptron and random forest techniques. Multiple classifiers were included to expand on the accuracy that can be achieved by an emotion detection system that could possibly be used to aid speaker authentication systems.

Multilayer Perceptron. The initial classifier selected for the purpose of identifying a portrayed emotion is the multilayer perceptron (MLP), a class of artificial neural networks (ANNs). The MLP is derived from a single-layer perceptron (SLP) which can be considered the most abstracted form of an ANN [11]. The learning process of an ANN entails determining values from weights by utilizing provided inputs and expected outputs, taking inspiration from the functionality of the human brain [27, p. 451]. Additionally, the performance of an ANN is measured by comparing actual outputs against expected outputs [27, p. 454].

The SLP consists of an input layer and an output layer that each contain multiple neurons, or nodes. The MLP is a layered feedforward ANN that consists of an input layer, one or more hidden layers, and an output layer. Each layer consists of multiple connected nodes, or neurons, that each have an assigned weight, as can be seen in Fig. 4.

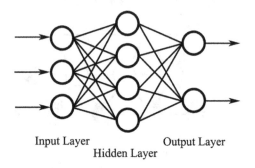

Input Layer   Output Layer

Hidden Layer

Fig. 4. Multilayer perceptron

The input nodes represent the features that were extracted, and the output nodes represent the identified emotion. Multiple factors could influence the performance of an MLP, including the training data, number of hidden layers, number of iterations, and learning approach [27, p. 454].

Random Forest. The additional classifier selected for this study was a random forest. This classifier consists of multiple Decision Trees, each representing a 'vote' towards a final outcome [3,18]. A decision tree takes the form of a flowchart structure, consisting of root nodes, branches, and leaf nodes [18]. The root nodes represent the provided features, the branches represent decision rules, and the leaf nodes represent the determined outcome. Similarly to an MLP, the decision tree predicts an outcome based on the provided data and measures performance by comparing the actual outcome to the expected outcome. A random forest utilizes multiple decision trees because a single decision tree often develop a bias towards the provided training data. Assigning a different combination of the provided features to each tree results in a high variance, and low bias within the random forest [22]. Each tree results in a determined outcome, the combination of which is averaged and captured as a final result.

5   Experiments Conducted

The experiments conducted during this study attempted to identify a portrayed emotion accurately through classification. This was accomplished by using the MLP and random forest classification techniques exclusively, maintaining a 75%/25% train/test ratio respectively. The audio samples selected for this study originated from the RAVDESS dataset. All the sound samples provided by 24 actors were included. However, the audio samples were reduced in length to three seconds. Additionally, only files associated with the predetermined emotions, namely neutral, happy, sad, angry, and fear were used. As these emotions were portrayed by actors, they can be considered synthetic. Nevertheless, tests utilizing these synthetic emotions were performed to prove the possibility of an emotionally aided speaker authentication system.

The creation of the RAVDESS dataset was followed by a validation process. This validation, performed by the creators of the dataset, included requesting 247 participants to identify portrayed emotions based on different categories. The participants were provided with 298 randomly selected samples from the created dataset, which included different combinations of voice and video samples. A further validation task initially required 72 participants, not including any of the previous participants, to identify portrayed emotions. Following a short break, the 72 participants were required to identify the same portrayed emotions, validating their initial identification. In the audio-only category, the RAVDESS dataset achieved 60% accuracy. This can be compared to the accuracy of similar datasets, such as, the CREMA-D, which achieved 41%, and the GEMEP, wwhich achieved 44% [17]. Considering this, the selected dataset proved adequate for the tests performed in this study.

This system was constructed using the Python 3 programming language as well as the Librosa and Sklearn libraries. Librosa added feature extraction functionality, and Sklearn added the implementation of the classifiers as well as the training and testing of the classifiers. The system extracts the selected features from the approved audio samples. These audio samples are approved only if they portray the selected emotion, which is determined by the audio sample file name. The collection of extracted features is then passed through the selected classifier. The MLP classifier was constructed as follows: The hidden layer size was set to 300. The max iterations were set to 500. The batch size was set to 256. Finally the learning rate, as defined by Sklearn, was set to 'Adaptive'. Additionally, the random forest was constructed as follows: The number of trees generated was set to 100. The number of features considered was set to the square root of the total number of features. Finally the maximum depth and maximum number of leaf nodes were not set.

Each experiment extracted a different combination of features, ensuring that each feature was tested unassisted. Each experiment portrayed an unassisted feature, resulting in five different experiments. The addition of features to each experiment resulted in different variation of the five experiments. Thus each classifier performed 21 experiments, resulting in a total of 42 experiments. Finally the average accuracy achieved for every combination of features was the result of three consecutive tests.

Table 1 and Table 2 are constructed in the same way and represent the results obtained from the MLP experiments and the random forest experiments, respectively

Table 1. MLP experiments

Experiment	MFCC	Chroma	Mel	Contrast	Tonnetz	# of Features	T1 Accuracy(%)	T2 Accuracy(%)	T3 Accuracy(%)	Avg Accuracy(%)
1A	1					40	72,1	72,8	67,3	70,8
1B	1	1				52	76,3	75,6	74,2	75,4
1C	1	1	1			180	71,4	71,4	74,2	72,4
1D	1	1	1	1		187	69,3	70,0	75,6	71,6
1E	1	1	1	1	1	193	75,0	73,5	68,7	72,4
2A		1				12	38,9	38,9	38,9	38,9
2B		1	1			140	69,3	70,0	69,3	69,6
2C			1	1	1	147	70,7	69,3	69,3	69,8
2D			1	1	1	153	68,0	66,6	67,3	67,3
3A			1			128	65,2	64,5	63,1	64,2
3B			1	1		135	70,0	66,6	68,0	68,2
3C			1	1	1	141	70,7	70,7	72,8	71,4
3D	1		1	1	1	181	75,0	78,4	72,1	75,2
4A				1		7	51,3	50,6	48,5	50,1
4B				1	1	13	53,4	47,8	48,5	49,9
4C	1			1	1	53	74,2	74,2	72,8	73,8
4D	1	1		1	1	65	75,6	81,2	75,0	77,2
5A					1	6	32,6	33,3	29,0	31,6
5B	1				1	46	70,0	75,0	74,2	73,1
5C	1	1			1	58	77,7	72,1	73,5	74,5
5D	1	1	1		1	186	77,7	74,2	71,4	74,5

The 'Experiment' column contains a two-character identifier consisting of experiment number and a letter indicating the variation, which is based on the combination of features implemented. The variations follow an alphabetical sequence as additional features are implemented. Variation 'A' contains the unassisted feature. This is followed by the addition of the next feature in the sequence. The sequence of features can be observed in the 'MFCC', 'Chroma', 'Mel', 'Contrast', and 'Tonnetz' columns. A '1' within these columns indicates the implementation of the corresponding feature. Experiment 1E is the only experiment that contains all the features, as it is not necessary to test this combination multiple times. The '# of Features' column indicates the total number of extracted features, which could help to determine the impact of the number of utilized features on the accuracy achieved. The accuracy achieved by each of the

Table 2. Random forest experiments

Experiment	MFCC	Chroma	Mel	Contrast	Tonnetz	# of Features	T1 Accuracy(%)	T2 Accuracy(%)	T3 Accuracy(%)	Avg Accuracy(%)
1A	1					40	64,3	67,1	65,2	65,5
1B	1	1				52	64,3	66,2	63,4	64,6
1C	1	1	1			180	61,5	57,4	60,6	59,8
1D	1	1	1	1		187	62,5	65,2	61,1	62,9
1E	1	1	1	1	1	193	62,0	59,2	60,6	60,6
2A		1				12	29,6	33,8	31,4	31,6
2B		1	1			140	58,8	55,5	60,1	58,1
2C		1	1	1		147	60,1	58,3	56,4	58,3
2D		1	1	1	1	153	58,8	57,4	57,8	58,0
3A			1			128	55,0	55,5	59,7	56,7
3B			1	1		135	56,9	58,8	56,4	57,4
3C			1	1	1	141	57,8	59,7	56,0	57,8
3D	1		1	1	1	181	62,0	59,7	56,0	59,2
4A				1		7	32,8	33,8	34,2	33,6
4B				1	1	13	30,0	33,3	31,0	31,4
4C	1			1	1	53	62,0	61,1	66,2	63,1
4D	1	1		1	1	65	59,7	64,8	60,1	61,5
5A					1	6	19,9	18,5	18,9	19,1
5B	1				1	46	61,5	66,2	62,9	63,5
5C	1	1			1	58	60,1	59,2	62,0	60,4
5D	1	1	1		1	186	61,5	62,9	61,5	62,0

three tests is presented in the 'T1 Accuracy (%)', 'T2 Accuracy (%)', and 'T3 Accuracy (%)' columns, respectively. Finally, the calculated average accuracy is presented in the 'Avg Accuracy (%)' column.

6   Discussion

When observing changes in accuracy caused by the addition of a certain feature, the experiment that included it as an unassisted feature cannot be included, as that experiment does not portray its addition. For example, the addition of the MFCC can be observed only in Experiments 3, 4, and 5, as Experiment 1 does not portray its addition, and Experiment 2 does not include it. The addition of tonnetz within random forest made an insignificant change in the accuracy achieved, reducing the accuracy of thee out of the four experiments that included the addition. Similarly, the addition of the tonnetz within the MLP reduced the accuracy in two out of four experiments. Both classifiers displayed a reduction in accuracy of just over two percent. The random forest showed an increase in accuracy in all three experiments wherein contrast was included, whereas the three MLP experiments resulted in an increase, no change, and a reduction in accuracy respectively. When the mel spectrogram was added in Experiment 2B, it led to a significant improvement in accuracy for both classifiers. This was most likely due to the poor accuracy achieved by the chroma feature when used exclusively. The random forest resulted in a reduced accuracy only when the chroma feature was implemented in the system. Conversely, the MLP achieved an increase in accuracy only when the chroma feature was implemented. Finally, the addition of the MFCC feature improved the average accuracy in every experiment of both classifiers. The most notable increase, which was over 40%, can be observed in both the Experiment 5B tests, wherein the only features utilized were the tonnetz and the MFCC.

The number of features extracted did not significantly influence the accuracy achieved. For example, of the MLP experiemnts, Experiment 5A achieved 31.7% accuracy by utilizing six features, whereas Experiment 4A achieved 50.2% accuracy by utilizing seven features. Similarly, Experiment 1A achieved 70.8% accuracy by utilizing 40 features, while Experiment 1E achieved 72,4% accuracy by utilizing 193 features. This statement can similarly be construed when observing the random forest experiments.

The highest accuracy achieved by the MLP system is occurred in Experiment 4D, which included all of the features except the mel constrast and obtained 77.3% accuracy. The highest accuracy achieved by the random forest system occurred in Experiment 1A, which included only MFCC and obtained 65.5% accuracy.

7   Conclusions and Future Work

The utilization of speaker authentication as a biometric authentication method may improve upon existing traditional authentication methods. However, the possibility of authenticating an individual under duress increases as speaker authentication systems become more reliant on accuracy. Implementing additional functionalities to authenticate individuals' emotions may prove as vital as increasing the accuracy of speaker authentication systems. In this study, the accuracy achieved when authenticating emotion reached 77.3%. Although this accuracy is not as high as that of speaker authentication systems, a 'fearful' authentication may result in steps being taken to reduce the possible damage that could be caused by an inauthentic individual.

The accuracy achieved when authenticating emotions shows that emotion detection should not be considered as a factor of authentication when allowing or denying access to an individual. In the event that an emotion detection system detects that an individual has been authenticated under duress, additional steps can be taken to reduce any possible damage. These steps may include requiring a second authentication, requiring a lower level of authentication, implementing additional monitoring, or placing an alert on the account. An emotion detection system may provide a valuable warning when a negative emotion is detected during authentication. However, this should be used merely as an aid and not as an end-all when making authentication decisions.

The current emotion detection system made use of three second sound samples and implemented the classifiers by means of Sklearn. A future system would test sound samples of multiple durations to identify the impact on the accuracy achieved. It should also use additional datasets such as TESS and SAVEE. Additional classifiers would also be implemented and compared with the existing two. These could include Support Vector Machine, Naive Bayes, and K-nearest Neighbors. Furthermore, the classifiers would be implemented using a different approach, as the Sklearn library does not support Deep Learning.

References

1. Al-Ali, A.K.H., Dean, D., Senadji, B., Chandran, V., Naik, G.R.: Enhanced forensic speaker verification using a combination of DWT and MFCC feature warping in the presence of noise and reverberation condition. IEEE Access **5**, 15400–15413 (2017)
2. Ambalakat, P.: Security of biometric authentication systems. In: 21st Computer Science Seminar, pp. 1–7 (2005)
3. Belgiu, M., Drăguţ, L.: Random forest in remote sensing: a review of applications and future directions. ISPRS J. Photogram. Remote Sens. **114**, 24–31 (2016)
4. Bhattacharyya, D., Ranjan, R., Alisherov, F., Choi, M., et al.: Biometric authentication: a review. Int. J. u- and e- Serv. Sci. Technol. **2**(3), 13–28 (2009)
5. Boles, A., Rad, P.: Voice biometrics: deep learning-based voiceprint authentication system. In: 12th System of Systems Engineering Conference (SoSE), pp. 1–6 (2017)
6. Das, R.K., Jelil, S., Prasanna, S.M.: Development of multi-level speech based person authentication system. J. Signal Process. Syst. **88**(3), 259–271 (2017)
7. De Ru, W.G., Eloff, J.H.: Enhanced password authentication through fuzzy logic. IEEE Expert **12**(6), 38–45 (1997)
8. Delgado, H., et al.: Further optimisations of constant q cepstral processing for integrated utterance and text-dependent speaker verification. In: SLT 2016: 2016 IEEE Spoken Language Technology Workshop (SLT), pp. 179–185 (2016)
9. Eerola, T., Vuoskoski, J.K.: A comparison of the discrete and dimensional models of emotion in music. Psychol. Music **39**(1), 18–49 (2011)
10. Harte, C.A., Sandler, M.B., Gasser, M.: Detecting harmonic change in musical audio. In: AMCMM 2006: Proceedings of the 1st ACM Workshop on Audio and Music Computing for Multimedia, pp. 21–26 (2006)
11. Heidari, A.A., Faris, H., Aljarah, I., Mirjalili, S.: An efficient hybrid multilayer perceptron neural network with grasshopper optimization. Soft Comput. **23**(17), 7941–7958 (2019)

12. Humphrey, E.J., Cho, T., Bello, J.P.: Learning a robust tonnetz-space transform for automatic chord recognition. In: 2012 IEEE International Conference on Acoustics, Speech and Signal Processing (ICASSP), pp. 453–456 (2012)

13. Jang, D., Jin, M., Yoo, C.D.: Music genre classification using novel features and a weighted voting method. In: 2008 IEEE International Conference on Multimedia and Expo, pp. 1377–1380 (2008)

14. Jiang, D.N., Lu, L., Zhang, H.J., Tao, J.H., Cai, L.H.: Music type classification by spectral contrast feature. In: Proceedings of IEEE International Conference on Multimedia and Expo, vol. 1, pp. 113–116 (2002)

15. Jiang, N., Grosche, P., Konz, V., Müller, M.: Analyzing chroma feature types for automated chord recognition. In: AES 42nd International Conference on Semantic Audio (2011)

16. Kinnunen, T., et al.: Utterance verification for text-dependent speaker recognition: a comparative assessment using the reddots corpus. In: Interspeech 2016, pp. 430–434, September 2016

17. Livingstone, S.R., Russo, F.A.: The Ryerson audio-visual database of emotional speech and song (RAVDESS): a dynamic, multimodal set of facial and vocal expressions in north American English. PloS ONE **13**(5), e0196391 (2018)

18. Masetic, Z., Subasi, A.: Congestive heart failure detection using random forest classifier. Comput. Methods Programs Biomed. **130**, 54–64 (2016)

19. Müller, M., Ewert, S.: Chroma toolbox: matlab implementations for extracting variants of chroma-based audio features. In: Conference: Proceedings of the 12th International Society for Music Information Retrieval Conference, pp. 215–220 (2011)

20. Müller, M., Kurth, F., Clausen, M.: Audio matching via chroma-based statistical features. In: ISMIR (2005)

21. Odu, T., Idachaba, F.: A review of the fingerprint, speaker recognition, face recognition and iris recognition based biometric identification technologies. In: World Congress on Engineering 2011, July 2011

22. Pavey, T.G., Gilson, N.D., Gomersall, S.R., Clark, B., Trost, S.G.: Field evaluation of a random forest activity classifier for wrist-worn accelerometer data. J. Sci. Med. Sport **20**(1), 75–80 (2017)

23. Ramgire, J.B., Jagdale, S.M.: A survey on speaker recognition with various feature extraction and classification techniques. Int. Res. J. Eng. Technol. (IRJET) **3**(4), 709–712 (2016)

24. Sarkar, A.K., Tan, Z.H.: Incorporating pass-phrase dependent background models for text-dependent speaker verification. Comput. Speech Lang. **47**, 259–271 (2018)

25. Sarria-Paja, M., Falk, T.H.: Fusion of auditory inspired amplitude modulation spectrum and cepstral features for whispered and normal speech speaker verification. Comput. Speech Lang. **45**, 437–456 (2017)

26. Sell, G., Clark, P.: Music tonality features for speech/music discrimination. In: 2014 IEEE International Conference on Acoustics, Speech and Signal Processing (ICASSP), pp. 2489–2493 (2014)

27. Taud, H., Mas, J.: Multilayer perceptron (MLP). In: Geomatic Approaches for Modeling Land Change Scenarios, pp. 451–455 (2018)

28. Thullier, F.: A Practical Application of a Text-Independent Speaker Authentication System on Mobile Devices. Ph.D. thesis, University of Quebec at Chicoutimi, February 2016

29. Thullier, F., Bouchard, B., Menelas, B.A.J.: A text-independent speaker authentication system for mobile devices. Cryptography **1**(3), 16 (2017)

30. Wang, J.C., Wang, C.Y., Chin, Y.H., Liu, Y.T., Chen, E.T., Chang, P.C.: Spectral-temporal receptive fields and MFCC balanced feature extraction for robust speaker recognition. Multimedia Tools Appl. **76**(3), 4055–4068 (2017)
31. Wang, Y.B.: The classification of music styles on the basis of spectral contrast features. J. Korea Soc. Comput. Inf. **22**(1), 8–13 (2017)

Identification of Information Security Controls for Fitness Wearable Manufacturers

Sophia Moganedi[1,2(⊠)] and Dalenca Pottas[1]

[1] Nelson Mandela University, Port Elizabeth, South Africa
s209078565@mandela.ac.za, Dalenca.Pottas@Mandela.ac.za
[2] CSIR, Pretoria, South Africa
smoganedi@csir.co.za

Abstract. Statista suggests that there would be 368.2 million wearables shipped globally in 2020 with a projection of 500 million by 2024. These predictions are becoming a reality considering the fast growing of Intent of Things (IoT) domain. These wearables come in different forms, shapes, and sizes. The existence of fitness wearables encourages people to participate in a healthy lifestyle through tracking of health and fitness-related activities. The functionality of these devices includes gathering, processing, transmitting, and storing user data. However, these devices carry with them vulnerabilities that can negatively affect the security and privacy of a user. Therefore, the primary objective of this study is to identify security controls to mitigate the vulnerabilities that affect fitness wearables from a security and privacy perspective. However, to identify these security controls, the researcher firstly identifies the vulnerabilities affecting these fitness wearables. This study executed a methodology in two stages. The first stage conducted a literature review to identify the vulnerabilities affecting fitness wearables and related components within the ecosystem of fitness wearables. The second state follows a systematic analysis approach to identify security controls for the fitness wearable manufacturers to mitigate these vulnerabilities. The final output of this study indicates the security complexities surrounding the fitness wearables by presenting the study limitations.

Keywords: Fitness wearables · Vulnerabilities · Security controls · Internet of Things

1 Introduction

Fitness wearables are a part of the bigger interconnected world of the Internet of Things (IoT) [1, 2]. A fitness wearable is defined as a wireless sensor that is embedded in a device and can be worn on the body by the user [3]. This device incorporates a variety of capabilities including gathering, processing, transmitting, and storing user data [4, 5]. Fitness wearables are manufactured and put into the market to encourage users to participate in self-care through excises and health monitoring efforts [6].

The popularity of these fitness wearables is influenced by the increasing interest in self-tracking notion, where users can track and monitor their daily fitness-related

H. Venter et al. (Eds.): ISSA 2020, CCIS 1339, pp. 112–128, 2020.
https://doi.org/10.1007/978-3-030-66039-0_8

activities [7–10]. However, the growing popularity of fitness wearables and their use poses security concerns [11]. These security concerns around the fitness wearables are not surprising, given the fact that these devices gather real-time data that tends to be at a personal and detailed level [12]. Hence, the discussions around personal privacy increase these concerns as users lose control of the data privacy [13].

The remainder of this paper is organised as follows: Sect. 2 presents the methodology employed in this study. Section 3 presents the findings and the output of this study, which is the information security controls for the fitness wearable manufacturers to mitigate the vulnerabilities affecting the fitness wearables ecosystem. Section 4 presents the limitation of this study and make recommendations for future research based on the limitations discussed. The limitations opens an opportunity to further this study. Section 4 concludes the study and highlight the contribution made by this study.

2 Methodology

This section discusses the methodology followed by this study. This study executed the methodology in two stages to achieve the identified objective/s. In Stage 1, the researcher conducted a literature review to identify vulnerabilities that affect fitness wearables from a security and privacy perspective. Stage 2 employed a systematic analysis approach to identify security controls for the fitness wearable manufacturers to mitigate the vulnerabilities. Subsections 2.1 and Subsect. 2.2 provide a more detailed discussion on each of these stages.

2.1 Stage 1: Literature Review

This subsection discusses the literature review followed to identify the vulnerabilities affecting fitness wearables from a security and privacy perspective.

Firstly, the researcher adopted the Open Web Application Security Project (OWASP) Internet of Things (IoT) 2018 project as a baseline to identify the vulnerabilities that exist in the IoT domain. This project started in 2014 to assist developers, manufacturers, and users to make better security decisions when designing and using IoT systems [14]. The OWASP IoT project released the top 10 IoT vulnerabilities that the broader IoT academic community endorses. Hence, the adoption by this study.

The literature identified the "Lack of Erasing Personal Data" as an additional vulnerability that is significant to the IoT domain and yet not on the OWASP list [15]. Therefore, this study will be focusing on eleven (11) vulnerabilities. The conducting of the literature review was to find earlier and recent published work that presents these vulnerabilities from the fitness wearable context. This study conducted comparison analysis of three source to understand the approach followed to identify vulnerabilities and security controls to mitigate those vulnerabilities. The findings from this analysis indicates that each of the sources follows the risk assessment approach which is the well-known approach for identifying vulnerabilities and security controls in an organizational context.

Furthermore, through the literature, the researcher identifies the components that these vulnerabilities affect within the fitness wearable ecosystem. Figure 1 below depicts the fitness wearables ecosystem to demonstrate the fitness wearables and their related components for the full fitness tracking and monitoring functionality. This study notes that there are various mode of communication and additional functionalities found in different fitness wearable brands and such include Apple smart watch that offers the fitness functionality and inbuilt cellular access. However, this study is focusing on general fitness wearables that offer fitness functionality and not on a specific brand or additional functionality within the wearables. A letter as presented in Fig. 1 represents each component in the ecosystem.

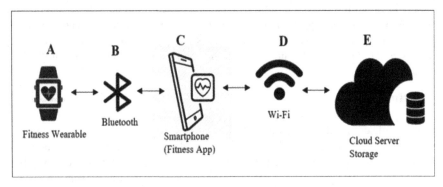

Fig. 1. Fitness wearables ecosystem

2.2 Stage-2: Analysis Approach

This subsection discusses the analysis approach followed in this study. The purpose of this analysis is to identify a set of security controls for the fitness wearable manufacturers to mitigate the vulnerabilities affecting the fitness wearable ecosystem. Therefore, the identification of these security controls is done by determining the relevance of the security controls in the context of this study. In addition to determining the relevance, the identification aims to select critical security controls that will provide a high impact when implemented. These security controls are for fitness wearable manufacturers to mitigate the list of these vulnerabilities identified through the OWASP IoT Project.

The execution of this analysis was in a two-phased approach. This study used the NIST SP800-53 revision 5 to identify the security controls for mitigating the list of vulnerabilities identified. Figure 2 below depicts a high-level process followed in each phase. Each phase presents the steps involved. The subsections below presents a more detailed discussion on each the phases.

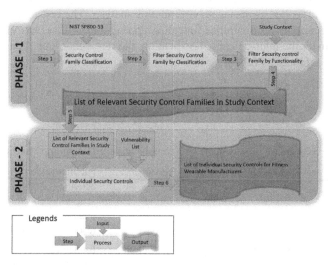

Fig. 2. High-Level Two-phased APPROACH

Phase 1 Analysis

Phase 1 aims to identify the relevant security control families from the NIST. The NIST SP800-53 Rev 5 has 20 security control families and each consists of a set of security controls relating to the security functionality of that family. The main goal of Phase 1 is to identify the security control families that are relevant in the context of this study. However, Subsection A and Subsection B presents the two levels of relevance in the context of this study.

A. *Security Control Family Classification Filtering*

The first level of relevance focuses on whether the technical and operational aspect of the security control families are possible for implementation. The technical aspect focuses on the implementation of security measures before the fitness wearable and its related components are in the public market. While the operational aspect focuses on security measures to ensure that the fitness wearable and related components are secure when used in the market and their security posture can always be improved. As a result, the researcher adopted the classification of security control family from NIST SP800-53 revision 1. The reason for adopting this classification from the earliest revision 1 (Rev 1) of NIST is simply because the latest revision (Rev 5) of NIST does not provide such classification. Furthermore, the earliest revision (Rev 1) provides only seventeen (17) security control families; therefore, the researcher had to classify the remaining security control families that did not exist in Rev 1. The additional classification emerges from the overall functionality of the security control family.

The NIST provides three classifications for the security control families. These classifications are namely: Management, Operational, and Technical. The selection of the security control families that are relevant in the context of this study is on two classifications, which are technical and operational. As a result, this study excludes security control family classified as management from this analysis. The researcher started with twenty (20) security control families, and after filtering out all the security control families falling under the management classification, the researcher identified sixteen (16) security control families (Table 1).

Table 1. NIST SP800-53 security control families

Selected	Security control family name	Classification	Description/Functionality
✓	Access Control	Technical	Facilitates the permitted activities of legitimate users' access systems to preventing unauthorised access to system resources
✓	Awareness and Training	Operational	Implements security awareness and training to information system users
✓	Audit and Accountability	Technical	Determines audit events, ensure recording of events, and ensure reliability and protection.
	Assessment, Authorization, and Monitoring	Management	Assesses the current security posture of an organization as well as assessing the potential security risks.
✓	Configuration Management	Operational	Ensures critical assets are properly configured at all times and configuration changes are only restricted to authorised users
✓	Contingency Planning	Operational	Ensures the continuity of critical operations and restoration of information systems during compromises
✓	Identification and Authentication	Technical	Ensures claimed user identity and rights to access the information system
✓	Incident Management	Operational	Implement an organised approach to address and manage the aftermath of security incidents.

(*continued*)

Table 1. (*continued*)

Selected	Security control family name	Classification	Description/Functionality
✓	Maintenance	Operational	Ensures sustainability in the capability of information systems to provide the designated services
✓	Media Protection	Operational	Ensures the security of digital and non-digital media
✓	Physical and Environment Protection	Operational	Aim to prevent the loss or damage to information assets and interruption to the business activities from unauthorized access
	Planning	Management	Determines security requirements and identify security controls. It includes describing how security controls will meet those security requirements
✓	Personnel Security	Operational	Ensures that individuals within an organisation are not posing security risks to the organisation and the information systems
	Risk Assessment	Management	Identifies and assesses the security risks in an organisation and information systems. This is to determine the likelihood and the impact of security harm
	System and Services Acquisition	Management	Focuses on new system design methods, major changes in existing systems, support, resource allocation, system documentation, and system minimum requirements
✓	System and Communication Protection	Technical	Focuses on the protection of information systems and the communication processes
✓	System and Information Integrity	Operational	Aim to protect information systems, communication, and preserve the integrity of information

(*continued*)

Table 1. (*continued*)

Selected	Security control family name	Classification	Description/Functionality
✓	Program Management	Operational	Focuses on managing security-related programs in the organisation
✓	PII Processing and Transparency	Operational	Focuses on the processing of PII, which includes gathering, processing, transmitting, storing, disclosure, and disposal of such information
✓	Supply Chain Risk Management	Operational	Focuses on managing day to day risks that come with the supply chain in an organisation

B. *Security Control Family Functionality*

The functionality of a particular security control family in the context of this study determines the second level of relevance. These criteria determines the inclusion or exclusion of the security control families. The focus was on filtering out security control families that are not relevant in the context of this study addressing fitness wearables and their related components. The previous subsection identified relevant security control families based on the technical and operational classifications. However, some of these security control families were irrelevant in the context of this study.

The **Awareness and Training** security control family focuses on training users in an organisational context and as a result, this security control family is irrelevant in the context of this study.

Another example of a security control family that falls under a relevant classification but is irrelevant in the context of this study is the **Physical and Environmental Protection** security control family. This security control family focuses on ensuring the protection of an organisation in terms of actual physical security to protect the physical infrastructure. This is relevant in the context of an organisation but is irrelevant in the context of fitness wearables and their related components. Table 2 presents the excluded security control families. These exclusions were because these security control families are applicable in an organisational context but not in the context of this study. The exclusion of a security control family excludes the individual security controls within that family.

At the end of Phase 1, the researcher had six security control families that are relevant in the context of this study addressing the fitness wearables and their related components. Table 3 presents these security control families.

Phase 2 Analysis

In Phase 2, the researcher focused on identifying individual security controls within security control families for the fitness wearable manufacturers to mitigate the list of vulnerabilities.

Table 2. Filtering security controls: based on study context

Security Control Family Name	Classification
Access Control	Technical
Awareness and Training	Operational
Audit and Accountability	Technical
Configuration Management	Operational
Contingency Planning	Operational
Identification and Authentication	Technical
Incident Management	Operational
Maintenance	Operational
Media Protection	Operational
Physical and Environment Protection	Operational
Personnel Security	Operational
System and Communication Protection	Technical
System and Information Integrity	Operational
Program Management	Operational
PII Processing and Transparency	Operational
Supply Chain Risk Management	Operational

Table 3. Relevant security control families for study context

Security control family name	Classification
Access Control	Technical
Audit and Accountability	Technical
Identification and Authentication	Technical
System and Communication Protection	Technical
System and Information Integrity	Operational
PII Processing and Transparency	Operational

For this phase, the researcher took the list of vulnerabilities affecting various components within the fitness wearables ecosystem as an input into this Phase 2 analysis. In addition to the list of vulnerabilities, the researcher also took the six (6) security control families that were an output in Phase 1 to be an input in Phase 2. The purpose of using these two outputs as an input in this Phase 2 is to identify relevant security controls for the fitness wearable manufactures to mitigate these vulnerabilities.

This phase executes a more detailed analysis by going through each security control family and identifying individual security controls that are relevant in the context of the vulnerabilities and the manufacturer can use to mitigate these vulnerabilities. Furthermore, the identification of the security controls for the mitigation of the vulnerabilities is in three levels. The first level identifies security controls that will mitigate the vulnerability; the second level identifies security controls that will strengthen the security control identified for the first level. Finally, the third level identifies security controls as reactive measure in case of an incident. This structure presents Security control, Related Control, and Control enhancements. According to NIST, the "Security Control" as the main security control and recommends related controls to strengthen the main security control. These related controls are controls from other security control families. Lastly, the control enhancements are within the main security controls, which NIST recommends to strengthen the main Security controls. However, for this study, the adoption of the presentation structure is different. The "related controls" are not necessarily those recommended by the NIST, but they fit the context of this study and the same applies to the "control enhancements".

Table 4 presents the identification of individual security controls. The study presents one example of vulnerability with mitigation security controls and the affected components. The components A, B, C and E are those presented in Fig. 1. The summary later is the study presents the rest of the vulnerabilities with their identified security controls.

3   Findings and Presentation

This section presents the main contribution of this study, which is the result of the methodology discussed in the previous section.

3.1   Vulnerabilities Affecting Fitness Wearables

This section presents a brief discussion and presents the vulnerabilities that affect fitness wearables and related components. The purpose of this discussion to illustrate how each vulnerability as described by the OWASP IoT project affects the fitness wearable and related components. The literature supports and validate the applicability of these vulnerabilities in the context of the fitness wearables.

Table 5 below presents the list of vulnerabilities adopted from the OWASP IoT project and a mapping of each vulnerability to the components it affects. A letter as seen in Fig. 2 above represents each affected component. However, this study excludes the component labeled "D" from this analysis as its security requirements are not the responsibility of the fitness wearable manufacture.

3.2   Identification of Security Controls

There are several internationally known security control standards, frameworks, and guidelines that provide a huge list of security controls that can be used to mitigate security risks [56]. These security control standards, frameworks, and guidelines include the International Organization for Standardization and International Electrotechnical Commission (ISO/IEC), Control Objective for Information and Related Technology (COBIT), and National Institute of Standards and Technology (NIST), just to name a few. However, for this study, the researcher selected the NIST as a baseline to identify

Table 4. Identification of security controls for insecure data transfer snd storage

Components	Vulnerability	Security control family	Security controls	Reason for selection/Recommendation reason
A, B, C, E	Insecure Data Transfer and Storage	SC	[SC-8] Transmission Confidentiality and Integrity	**SC-8** recommends the implementation of an encryption mechanism to protect the confidentiality and integrity of information as it is being transmitted [16]. Encryption ensures the security of the information [17]
			[SC-20] Protection of Information at Rest	**SC-28** recommends the implementation of an encryption mechanism to protect the integrity of information at rest. This will prevent unauthorized disclosure or modification of information [16]. The encryption technique has proven to increase the level of data protection for assuring integrity and availability [18]
			[SC-13] Cryptographic Protection	**SC-18** supports different security solutions that include the protection of information. The encryption technique help to maintain the confidentiality, integrity, and availability of the data [19].
			[SC-23] Session Authenticity	**SC-23** focuses on protecting the authenticity of communication sessions. Fitness wearable ecosystem allow data to travel from one point to another, protection of communication session ensures confidentiality and integrity

Table 5. List of vulnerabilities affecting fitness wearables and related components

Components	Vulnerabilities	Cause/Impact of the vulnerability
A, C, E	Weak, Guessable, or Hardcoded Passwords	Unchangeable credentials that are shipped with the devices which include a backdoor to firmware or software can be used to grand unauthorised access to the device [14, 20–27]
A, C, E	Insecure Network Services	Unneeded and insecure services can compromise the confidentiality, integrity, and availability of the data [14, 28–30]
A, B, C, E	Insecure Ecosystem Interface	Any insecure component within the infrastructure can be used to compromise the entire ecosystem [14, 31–34]
A, B, C	Lack of Secure Update Mechanisms	Lack of the ability to update the devices in a secure manner. Security updates are not validated and encrypted [14, 31, 35]
A, C	Use of Insecure or Outdated Components	Devices operating from unpatched or outdated software components and libraries lead to an easy compromise. [32, 36–39]
A, B, C, E	Insufficient Privacy Protection	Storing of user's data insecurely, improperly or without the consent of the user in any components [2, 27, 48, 40–47]
A, B, C, E	Insecure Data Transfer and Storage	Lack of encryption or access control to data at any point within the ecosystem [27, 42, 53].
A, C	Lack of Device Management	Devices deployed lack the security support in an operational environment [14]
A, C	Insecure Default Settings	Devices shipped with default settings can be easily reconfigured for malicious purposes [33, 51, 52]
A, C	Lack of Physical Hardening	Lack of physical hardening measures will enable a potential malicious attacker to gain sensitive data [23, 38, 53]
A, C, E	Lack of Erasing Personal Data	There is a lack of the ability to allow for wiping off the gathered data in case of theft, loss or reselling of the device [15, 58]

security controls that will be relevant in the context of this study, which addresses the fitness wearables and related components.

The purpose of selecting the NIST standard as a baseline is because, this standard is a combination of several internationally recognized standards and best practices which include the ISO/IEC 27002 [57]. The specific NIST standard referred to by this study is NIST Special Publication 800-53. This publication presents security and privacy controls that are published for Federal Information Systems and Organisation [58].

Although the researcher identified one standard to use for identification these security controls, this standard presents a long list of security controls to select from, and selecting the best set of security controls is a challenge [59]. The identification of the most effective security controls has always been problematic and many approaches and techniques have developed over time to do this in the most effective manner possible [59,[60]. Barnard and Von Solms [59], acknowledges the existence of baseline manuals, however, they argue that these baseline manuals provide a little guidance on how to determine the best set of security controls to provide adequate security. Therefore, with this little guidance provided in the baseline manuals, there is a high potential of selecting irrelevant security controls and excluding the relevant ones [59, 61].

The literature recognizes the use of various mechanisms to identify a set of security controls to provide adequate security against security risks. However, such mechanisms are relevant in the context of implementing adequate security in an organisation. Hence, such mechanisms are irrelevant in the context of this study, which addresses the fitness wearables.

Table 6 below presents a summary of all the identified security controls for fitness wearable manufactures to mitigate each vulnerability.

Table 6. Summary of the identified security controls

Components	Vulnerabilities	Security controls	Related security control	Reactive security control	NIST supportive documents
A, C, E	Weak, Guessable, or Hardcoded Passwords	[IA-5], [SI-3], [SI-7]	[AC-7], [IA-9]		NIST SP800-118
A, C, E	Insecure Network Services	[SC-13], [SC-23]	[SC-28] [SC-8]		NIST SP800-123
A, B, C, E	Insecure Ecosystem Interface	[IA-9], [IA-3], [SC-8], [SC-13], [SC-23], [SC-28]	[IA-5]		NIST SP800-183

(*continued*)

Table 6. (*continued*)

Components	Vulnerabilities	Security controls	Related security control	Reactive security control	NIST supportive documents
A, B, C	Lack of Secure Update Mechanisms	[SI-2], [SI-3], [SI-7]	[SC-13], [SC-13]		NIST SP800-123
A, C	Use of Insecure or Outdated Components	[SI-2], [SI-3], [SI-7]	[SC-13]		NIST SP800-123
A, B, C, E	Insufficient Privacy Protection	[PT-2], [PT-3], [PT-4], [PT-5] [PT-6], [SC-28], [SC-42]	[SC-13], [SI-18]	[AU-10], [AU-9]	NIST SP800-122
A, B, C, E	Insecure Data Transfer and Storage	[SC-8], [SC-28], [SC-13]	[SI-18]		NIST SP800-111
A, C	Lack of Device Management	[SI-2]	[SC-13], [SI-3], [SI-7]		NIST SP800-124
A, C	Insecure Default Settings	[IA-5]	[SC-13]		NIST SP800-123
A, C	Lack of Physical Hardening	[IA-5], [AC-11] [SI-2]	[IA-11]		NIST SP800-123
A, C, E	Lack of Erasing Personal Data	[AC-4], [SI-19]	[SI-21]	[AU-3], [AU-10] [AU-11], [AU-8] [AU-9]	NIST SP800-88

4 Limitation and Future Research

This study identified a set of security controls to mitigate the list of vulnerabilities adopted from the OWASP IoT project. Through the NIST SP800-53, the researcher identifies the security controls that were relevant in the context of this study. However, the limitation of this study is the evaluation process of these security controls. Through the literature, it was evident that selecting the best set of security controls can be a great challenge and there is a potential to include unnecessary security controls while excluding the important ones. This is due to the lack of guidelines for selecting the best security controls. Therefore, for future research purposes, this study foresees a need to conduct further research that will propose and develop an evaluation process or model or framework to evaluate these sets of security controls for completeness, accuracy, and to verify if they will be implementable in the context of fitness wearables.

5 Conclusion

The fast growing market of fitness wearables has changed the way people are viewing their health habits. These devices motivate people to track and monitor their health habits daily. However, the fast growing of these fitness wearables has shown security and privacy to be an issue to this day. This study identified vulnerabilities and security controls for the mitigation of these vulnerabilities. The identification of security controls will enable the fitness wearable manufacturers to mitigate the most common vulnerabilities that affect the fitness wearables and entire IoT domain. Furthermore, these security controls identified simplifies the selection and implementation. Each security control mitigates a particular vulnerability, and the fitness wearable component affected.

References

1. Wei, J.: How wearables intersect with the cloud and the internet of things: Considerations for the developers of wearables. In: IEEE Consumer Electronics Magazine, pp. 53–56 (2014)
2. Zhou, W., Piramuthu, S.: Security/privacy of wearable fitness tracking IoT devices. In: 2014 9th Iberian Conference Information systems and Technologies (CISTI) (2014)
3. Britton, K.E.: IoT big data: consumer wearables data privacy and security. Landside A Publ. ABA Sect. Intellect. Prop. Law **8**(2), 1–8 (2015)
4. Bond-myatt, C.: Health wearables. In: Apps & Information Protection (2015)
5. Hiremath, S., Yang, G., Mankodiya, K.: Wearable internet of things : concept, architectural components and promises for person-centered healthcare. In: 2014 4th International Conference on Wireless Mobile Communication and Healthcare - "Transforming Healthcare Through Innovations in Mobile and Wireless Technologies" (MOBIHEALTH), pp. 304–307 (2014)
6. Bender, C.G., Hoffstot, J.C., Combs, B.T., Hooshangi, S., Cappos, J.: Measuring the fitness of fitness trackers. In: 2017 IEEE Sensors Applications Symposium (SAS) (2017)
7. Das, A.K., Pathak, P.H., Chuah, C., Mohapatra, P.: Uncovering privacy leakage in BLE network traffic of wearable fitness trackers. In: HotMobile'16 Proceedings of the 17th International Workshop on Mobile Computing Systems and Applications, pp. 99–104 (2016)
8. Michaelis, J.R., et al.: Describing the user experience of wearable fitness technology through online product reviews. In: Proceedings of the Human Factors Ergonomics Society 2016 Annual Meeting 1073, vol. 60, no. 1, pp. 1073–1077 (2016)
9. Lunney, A., Cunningham, N.R., Eastin, M.S.: Wearable fitness technology: A structural investigation into acceptance and perceived fitness outcomes. Comput. Human Behav. **65**, 114–120 (2016)
10. Anzaldo, D.: Wearable sports technology – market landscape and computer SoC trends. In: 2015 International SoC Design Conference (ISOCC), pp. 217–218 (2015)
11. Popat, K.A., Sharma, P.: Wearable computer applications a future perspective. Int. J. Eng. Innov. Technol. **3**(1), 213–217 (2013)
12. Martini, P.: A secure approach to wearable technology. Netw. Secur. **2014**(10), 15–17 (2014)

13. Huang, K.-C., Hsu, J.-F.: Balance between privacy protecting and selling user data of wearable devices. In: 14th International Telecommunications Society (ITS) Asia-Pacific Regional Conference: "Mapping ICT into Transformation for the Next Information Society" (2017)
14. OWASP, "OWASP Internet of Things Top 10 2018" (2018)
15. Bhattacharya, S.: The 10 Internet of Things Security Vulnerabilities (2019). https://resources. infosecinstitute.com/the-top-ten-iot-vulnerabilities/#gref. [Accessed: 20-Jun-2019]
16. Thambiraja, E., Ramesh, G., Umarani, R.: A survey on various most common encryption techniques. Int. J. Adv. Res. Comput. Sci. Softw. Eng. 2(7), 226–233 (2012)
17. Justin, J.M., Manimurugan, S.: A survey on various encryption techniques. Int. J. Soft Comput. Eng. 2(1), 2231–2307 (2012)
18. Albugmi, A., Alassafi, M.O., Walters, R., Wills, G.: Data security in cloud computing. In: 5th International Conference on Future Generation Communication Technologies, FGCT 2016, pp. 55–59 (2016)
19. Kaur, G.: Efficient data confidentiality and portability in cloud storage. Int. J. Adv. Res. Comput. Sci. 9(2), 40 (2018)
20. Barcena, M.B., Wueest, C.: Insecurity in the Internet of Things (2015)
21. Lindqvist, U., Neumann, P.G.: Inside risks the future of the internet of things. Commun. ACM 60(2), 26–30 (2017)
22. Mendoza, F., et al.: Assessment of fitness tracker security: a case of study. In: Proceedings, UCAmI 2018 The 12th International Conference on Ubiquitous Computing and Ambient Intelligence (UCAmI 2018), vol. 2, p. 1235 (2018)
23. Ching, K.W., Singh, M.M.: Wearable technology devices security and privacy vulnerability analysis. Int. J. Netw. Secur. Its Appl. 8(3), 19–30 (2016)
24. Mnjama, J., Foster, G., Irwin, B.: A privacy and security threat assessment framework for consumer health wearables. In: Information Security for South Africa (ISSA) 2017 (2017)
25. Cisneros, R., Bliss, D., Garcia, M.: Password auditing applications. J. Comput. Sci. Coll. 21(4), 196–202 (2006)
26. Li, S., Romdhani, I., Buchanan, W.: Password pattern and vulnerability analysis for web and mobile applications. ZTE Commun. 14(S0), 32–36 (2016)
27. Saini, H., Saini, A.: Security mechanisms at different levels in cloud infrastructure. Int. J. Comput. Appl. 108(2), 1–6 (2014)
28. Fredric, P.: Top 10 IoT Vulnerabilties. NetworkWorld (2019). https://www.networkworld. com/article/3332032/top-10-iot-vulnerabilities.html. Accessed 09 Jun 2019
29. Drolet, M.: 7 potential security concerns for wearables (2016)
30. Hilts, A., Parsons, C., Knockel, J.: Every step you fake: a comparative analysis of fitness tracker privacy and security (2016)
31. Classen, J., Wegemer, D., Patras, P., Spink, T., Hollick, M.: Anatomy of a vulnerable fitness tracking system: dissecting the fitbit cloud, app, and firmware. Proc. ACM Interact. Mob. Wearable Ubiq. Technol. 2(1), 1–24 (2018)
32. Vaughn, G.: IoT Security Best Practices (2019)
33. Pathak, A.K.: Security challenges in Internet of Things (IoT). Int. J. Adv. Res. Comput. Sci. Softw. Eng. 7(6), 648–652 (2017)
34. Goyal, R., Dragoni, N., Spognardi, A.: Mind the tracker you wear - a security analysis of wearable health trackers. In: Proceeding SAC'16 Proceedings of the 31st Annual ACM Symposium on Applied Computing, pp. 131–136 (2016)
35. Airehrour, D., Gutierrez, J., Ray, S.K.: Secure routing for internet of things: a survey. J. Netw. Comput. Appl. 66, 198–213 (2016)
36. Karthik: List of IoT Vulnerabilities (2019). http://secureapplication.org/blog/blogReadMore. php?id=1230. Accessed 17 June 2019
37. SecurityInstituteInformation.in, "Security Challenges in securing IoT," (2019). http://inform ationsecurityinstitute.in/security-challenges-in-securing-iot/. Accessed 09 June 2019

38. Rahman, A.F.A., Daud, M., Mohamad, M.Z.: Securing sensor to cloud ecosystem using internet of things (IoT) security framework. In: ICC'16 Proceedings of the International Conference on Internet of things and Cloud Computing, pp. 1–5 (2016)

39. Rieck, J.: Attacks on Fitness Trackers Revisited : A Case-Study of Unfit Firmware Security, pp. 33–44 (2016)

40. Radomirovi´c, S.: Towards a model for security and privacy in the internet of things. In: 1st International workshop on the Security of the Internet of Things (2010)

41. Wicks, P., Chiauzzi, E.: 'Trust but verify' - five approaches to ensure safe medical apps. BMC Med. **13**(1), 1–5 (2015)

42. Arias, O., Wurm, J.: Privacy and security in Internet of Things and wearable devices. IEEE Trans. Multi-Scale Comput. Syst. **1**(2), 99–109 (2015)

43. Barcena, M., Wueest, C., Lau, H.: How safe is your quantified self? (2014)

44. Kumar, M.: Security issues and privacy concerns in the implementation of wireless body area network. In: Proceedings - 2014 13th International Conference on Information Technology, ICIT 2014, pp. 58–62 (2014)

45. Bouhenguel, R., Mahgoub, I., Mohammad, I.: Bluetooth security in wearable computing applications. In: 2008 International Symposium on High Capacity Optical Networks and Enabling Technologies, HONET 2008, pp. 182–186 (2008)

46. Alfaiate, J., Fonseca, J.: Bluetooth security analysis for mobile phones. In: Iberian Conference on Information Systems and Technologies, CISTI (2012)

47. Hale, M.L., Ellis, D., Gamble, R., Waler, C., Lin, J.: Secu wear: an open source, multi-component hardware/software platform for exploring wearable security. In: Proceedings - 2015 IEEE 3rd International Conference on Mobile Services, MS 2015, pp. 97–104 (2015)

48. Musolesi, M.: Big mobile data mining: Good or evil? IEEE Internet Comput. **18**(1), 78–81 (2014)

49. Segura Anaya, L.H., Alsadoon, A., Costadopoulos, N., Prasad, P.W.C.: Ethical implications of user perceptions of wearable devices. Sci. Eng. Ethics **24**(1), 1–28 (2017). https://doi.org/10.1007/s11948-017-9872-8

50. Addonizio, G.: The privacy risks surrounding consumer health and fitness apps, associated wearable devices, and HIPAA's limitations (2017_

51. Algan, B.: Continuous Security Validation. ISACA Now BLog (2019). https://www.isaca.org/resources/news-and-trends/isaca-now-blog/2019/continuous-security-validation. [Accessed: 18-May-2020]

52. Williams, P.A.H., McCauley, V.: Always connected: the security challenges of the healthcare Internet of Things. In: 2016 IEEE 3rd World Forum on Internet of Things, WF-IoT 2016, pp. 30–35 (2017)

53. Mahinderjit, M.S., Ching, K.W., Manaf, A.A.:A novel out-of-band biometrics authentication scheme for wearable devices. Int. J. Comput. Appl., 1–13 (2018)

54. Messerges, T.S., Dabbish, E.A., Sloan, R.H.: Examining smart-card security under the threat of power analysis attacks. IEEE Trans. Comput. **51**(5), 541–552 (2002)

55. R. Adhikari, D. Richards, and K. Scott, "Security and privacy issues related to the use of mobile health apps," in *Proceedings of the 25th Australasian Conference on Information Systems, ACIS 2014*, 2014

56. Breier, J., Hudec, L.: On selecting critical security controls. In: 2013 International Conference on Availability, Reliability and Security, pp. 582–588 (2013)

57. Huijben, K.: A lightweight, flexible evaluation framework to measure the ISO 27002 information security controls," Radboud University (2014)

58. Lord, N.: What is NIST SP 800–53? Definition and Tips for NIST SP 800-53 Compliance (2018). https://digitalguardian.com/blog/what-nist-sp-800-53-definition-and-tips-nist-sp-800-53-compliance. Accessed 28 June 2019

59. Barnard, L., Von Solms, R.: A formalized approach to the effective selection and evaluation of information security controls. Comput. Secur. **19**(2), 185–194 (2000)
60. Hasheminejad, S.M.H., Jalili, S.: Selecting proper security patterns using text classification. In: Proceedings - 2009 International Conference on Computational Intelligence and Software Engineering, CiSE 2009, pp. 1–5 (2009)
61. Otero, A.R.: An information security control assessment methodology for organizations. Nova Southeastern Univerrsity (2014)

A Critical Evaluation of Validation Practices in the Forensic Acquisition of Digital Evidence in South Africa

Jason Jordaan[1]([✉]) [iD] and Karen Bradshaw[2] [iD]

[1] DFIRLABS, East London, South Africa
jason@dfirlabs.com
[2] Rhodes University, Grahamstown, South Africa

Abstract. Accepted digital forensics practice requires the tools used in the forensic acquisition of digital evidence to be validated, meaning that the tools perform as intended. In terms of Sect. 15 of the Electronic Communications and Transactions Act 25 of 2002 in South Africa, validation would contribute to the reliability of the digital evidence. A sample of digital forensic practitioners from South Africa was studied to determine to what extent they make use of validated forensic tools during the acquisition process, and how these tools are proven to be validated. The research identified significant concerns, with no validation done, or no proof of validation done, bringing into question the reliability of the digital evidence in court. It is concerning that the justice system itself is not picking this up, meaning that potentially unreliable digital evidence is used in court.

Keywords: Digital forensics · Forensic acquisition · Forensic imaging · Write blocker · Validation

1 Introduction

Digital evidence is an integral part of almost all investigations conducted presently; these investigations are not limited to suspected criminal offenses, but also includes civil investigations and regulatory investigations. The Electronic Communications and Transactions Act, 25 of 2002 [1], states that a critical consideration of the courts when looking at digital evidence is the reliability of the digital evidence and how the integrity thereof was maintained. Digital forensics is a crucial discipline used to address this.

Many digital forensic practitioners rely on hardware and software tools to produce results, often without the knowledge of how those results are produced, which risks not only their professional reputations but also the potential successful outcome of the investigation they have worked on [2].

One of the crucial elements of the entire digital forensics process is that digital forensic practitioners should have detailed knowledge of the capabilities, limitations, and restrictions of the tools they use [3]. One of the significant challenges faced by digital forensic practitioners is how to assure the reliability of the forensic tools they

© Springer Nature Switzerland AG 2020
H. Venter et al. (Eds.): ISSA 2020, CCIS 1339, pp. 129–143, 2020.
https://doi.org/10.1007/978-3-030-66039-0_9

use, especially as a result of the reliance that is often placed on these tools by digital forensic practitioners [4].

The evidence acquisition process requires that the source media containing the digital evidence is duplicated bit by bit, ensuring that all the data is duplicated and that the duplication process itself does not alter the data in any way. Various hardware and software tools are used during this process, and all tools and instruments used in any forensic science process must perform their functions correctly and accurately. Forensic science, therefore, relies on validation, verification, and calibration testing processes to ensure that the tools used are functioning within acceptable standards.

Previous research into quality assurance practices in digital forensics in South Africa [5] identified tool validation as a general area of concern. In terms of the forensic acquisition of digital evidence, if the tools used to preserve the evidence were not proven to be valid, then the admissibility and weight of the digital evidence could be significantly affected.

2 The Forensic Acquisition Process

The first forensic task in digital forensics is to make a forensic image of the original media, preserving the digital evidence [6]. Forensic acquisitions can take place in a "dead" environment where the media to be acquired is removed from the host and is attached to another host with a write blocker to obtain a forensic image. They can also be done in a "live" environment where the media is connected to its host, and a forensic image is made of it while it is still connected to the host. A "live" environment is when the host device is still powered on and running when the forensic acquisition process takes place.

Live acquisitions have become standard practice due to issues such as encryption. Because this process will alter the original media, digital forensic practitioners need to be able to document these changes and explain them in court to ensure admissibility as required by the ACPO guidelines [7]. The forensic acquisition process is the process whereby digital evidence is preserved in a forensically and legally correct manner that is designed to prevent or minimize any alteration or modification of the source data [8]. This process is generally referred to as forensic imaging of the evidence [2].

The forensic acquisition process should change the original evidence as little as possible, and if changes do occur, these changes must be identified and documented and then assessed in the examination and analysis of the evidence [9].

The critical issue in the forensic acquisition process is that it preserves a complete and accurate representation of the original data and that the authenticity and integrity of the evidence can be validated [9].

2.1 Forensic Imaging

There are fundamentally two types of forensic imaging methods when dealing with media: making a forensic image of the entire physical media, or only of a logical volume [6]. A logical forensic image is usually made of an encrypted volume, while the media is connected to its host, and the volume is currently decrypted, or of a limited set of data from the media.

Perhaps the most crucial aspect of the forensic imaging process is the process of validating the data acquisition (which is not the same as validating the tools used). During the data validation process, a one-way hash calculation is performed on the original data being imaged using a recognized one-way hashing algorithm (such as SHA-256) to create a hash value, which functions as a type of digital fingerprint for that data. The one-way hash calculation is then performed on the data from the forensic image using the same hashing algorithm to create a hash value. If the hash values of the original data and the image match, then the forensic image is said to be a real "duplicate original" of the original data [6]. If they do not match, there has been a problem in the forensic imaging process, and the reliability of the forensic image could be brought into question. As a result of this, the reliability of the software or hardware forensic imager that creates the forensic image is crucial to ensure the admissibility of the digital evidence in court.

2.2 Write Blocking

A write blocker is a mechanism that intercepts write commands to media before they can be executed on the media, which prevents any alteration to the media. A hardware write blocker is a physical device in which media is connected to which intercepts and blocks any write commands, while a software write blocker configures media to be read-only, thereby preventing alteration.

The National Institute of Justice strongly recommends that write protection should be used, if available and applicable, when acquiring digital evidence, to preserve and protect the original evidence during the forensic imaging process [10].

A write blocker allows data to be read from a device or media but prevents any writes being made to that device or media. Hardware-based write blockers are preferred over software write blockers, but there are times when each has specific applications to which it is best suited [2].

A write blocker, whether implemented in hardware or software, is a crucial part of the forensic acquisition process, and as such, it must function correctly to preserve the original evidence as much as possible.

3   The Importance of Validation in the Forensic Acquisition Process

Digital forensic practitioners make extensive use of forensic software and hardware, and to ensure quality results, they need to satisfactorily answer several questions, such as whether the forensic software used has any undocumented "bugs" and whether the forensic hardware was performing correctly [11].

Science has the power to persuade in a court of law, and as such, the courts must assess the validity of a scientific process before accepting its result [12]. The power of science in a court of law arises as a result of the supposed objectivity of its methods [13]. In other words, the fact that evidence is scientific often adds weight to it in a court of law. A central assumption in this is the fact that the court of law assumes that the scientific evidence, such as that presented as a result of the digital forensics process, is produced through an objective scientific process using validated methods and tools.

Determining the reliability of forensic tools through validation and verification is a critical quality assurance practice in digital forensics. This is in line with the requirements of all forensic sciences, which require that the tools that are used must be trust-worthy. Validation is defined as the confirmation by examination and the provision of objective evidence that a tool functions correctly and as intended. Verification is defined as the confirmation of validation with laboratory tools [4].

Hardware and software tools can have defects, and the digital forensics community has a responsibility to identify these defects owing to the nature of forensic work undertaken by them, which must satisfy the most stringent standards to have value in a court of law [14]. It has been observed through interactions with many digital forensic practitioners that some forensic tool vendors promote the strengths of their tools while underplaying their weaknesses, which have included incomplete forensic acquisitions, amongst others. Digital forensic practitioners must apply due diligence to ensure that the tools used in the forensic acquisition process work correctly. This is best done through validation either by themselves or through a trusted testing process; merely relying on vendor assurances is a significant risk.

Digital forensic examiners should be rigorously questioned when testifying to ensure their credibility and that of their findings. Some of the questions that they should be asked in court include whether they have documentation demonstrating that the forensic software or hardware used was validated before their use [11].

Fundamentally, the importance of validation testing of the tools used in the forensic acquisition process, whether a write blocker or forensic imager, is that it establishes the reliability of the tools used to obtain the digital evidence that will be used in a court of law. If the reliability cannot be established, then the reliability of the evidence itself would potentially be brought into question.

In a South African context, the courts must consider Sect. 15(3) of the Electronic Communications and Transactions Act 25 of 2002 [1] to determine the evidential weight of digital evidence, and reliability is an aspect that must be satisfied. If the reliability of a tool used to acquire the digital evidence is challenged, and it cannot be countered through an objective means that it is valid and reliable, the court must consider this.

4 Validation Standards and Practices Relating to the Forensic Acquisition Process

Validation and verification standards and practices exist that apply to the various forensic tools that can be used in the forensic acquisition process. These include hardware or software write blockers, and forensic imaging software or hardware. Some are formally documented standards, while others are practices that have developed in an ad-hoc manner by the digital forensics' community of practitioners. It is critical to be able to verify the results of any digital forensics tool used so that the accuracy of the tool can be assured [15].

- A digital forensic tool validation process should involve the following [14]:
- acquisition of the forensic tool to be evaluated,
- identification of the specific functions of the forensic tool,
- development of test cases and reference sets to be used in the evaluation process,
- development of an acceptable desired standard for the results,
- execution of the tests and evaluation of the results, and release of the results of the evaluation.

It must be borne in mind that the development of extensive and exhaustive tests to validate and verify digital forensics tools is a lengthy and complicated process [4]. In addition to this, the ability to test digital forensic tools is often limited due to both time and financial constraints for many digital forensic practitioners [14]. In general, digital forensic practitioners have heavy workloads and variations in resources and skill levels, providing conditions that are conducive to errors occurring in digital forensic tool testing. As a result, the tests themselves may not be accurate [16].

4.1 National Institute of Standards and Technology Computer Forensics Tool Testing Project

The National Institute of Standards and Technology (NIST) has been one of the pioneering organizations trying to address the validation and verification of digital forensics tools through their Computer Forensics Tool Testing (CFTT) project. They have developed specific testing methodologies for write blockers and forensic imaging [4].

The NIST CFTT standards are very comprehensive, but the technical comprehensiveness of the testing criteria also means that testing is time-consuming and requires a high level of technical proficiency.

4.2 The Scientific Working Group on Digital Evidence

The Scientific Working Group on Digital Evidence (SWGDE) has also been working on issues about the validation and verification of digital forensics tools, and rather than develop specific testing methodologies as the NIST CFTT project has done, they have recommended general guidelines for validation testing. The SWGDE validation guidelines for digital forensic tools include defining the purpose and scope of the validation test, defining the requirements to be tested, determining the methodology to be used, selecting appropriate test scenarios, conducting the tests, and documenting the process [4]. It is recommended that validation testing should be performed whenever a new, revised, or reconfigured tool is introduced into the forensic process [17].

4.3 European Network of Forensic Science Institutes

The European Network of Forensic Science Institutes has published broad validation testing guidelines for forensic imaging, which recommend that the imaging tools be checked to ensure that they make no changes to the original media, that the imaging verification process is reliable, and that the audit or log functions of the tool are accurate and detailed. Regarding write blocking tools, all that they require is that they need to be tested to ensure that they do not change any data on the original media [18].

4.4 Dual Tool Validation

Dual tool verification is a process whereby two different digital forensics tools are used to confirm whether both tools produce the same result. After one tool has been used to obtain a particular outcome, the results should be verified by performing the same tasks with another similar forensic tool [6]. Cross-validation is a critical element of quality assurance in digital forensics and requires the findings of a digital forensic tool to be verified by another digital forensic tool. Making use of only one forensic tool (and therefore trusting it blindly) creates an opportunity for the opposing party to target the tool instead of the process.

There is, however, a logical flaw in the concept of dual tool validation. What if both tools that are used in a dual tool validation do not work correctly? Unless the tool used to compare against is known to be functioning correctly and reliably, one cannot say with certainty that the tool it is being compared to is functioning correctly either. If one does make use of the dual tool validation method, then the tool that is used for comparison purposes should at least have been independently validated to ensure a measure of reliability.

4.5 Vendor Validation

There is a heavy reliance on digital forensic tools in the practice of digital forensics, and this reliance often hinges on blind faith that the specific tool works. This has led to industry myths that certain of these tools have been accepted by the courts and are thus court validated. Vendors, who are often protective of their commercial market share, have not officially published error rates for their digital forensic tools, or the exact reasons for minor and major version changes [19].

A problem with vendor validation is that it is generally undocumented and not proven publicly, except through comments, which are mostly hearsay on the bulletin boards of the vendors themselves [4].

5   Forensic Acquisition Tool Validations in South Africa

The research makes use of a structured questionnaire to collect quantitative data from South African digital forensic practitioners for analysis. Quantitative research is appropriate when trying to identify trends and generalizations that can be applied to a whole population [20].

Owing to practical issues such as the nature of the research and the time available to conduct the research, the research was limited in the following respect. The exact size of the population of digital forensic practitioners in South Africa is not known. As a result, the sample size needed to ensure that the sample is statistically representative so that generalizations can be made regarding the entire population of digital forensic practitioners in South Africa, could not be accurately determined.

In conducting this research, South African digital forensic practitioners were identified using two methods to identify potential respondents. Email invitations were sent to the managers/heads of the various digital forensic capacities within all state institutions with a digital forensics capacity, as well as to private sector organizations having a digital forensics capacity, requesting that the invitation be forwarded to all of their employees asking for their participation in the survey. In total, emails were sent to six state institutions and 19 private organizations. The researchers then conducted a search using LinkedIn[1] to identify all individuals in South Africa who were employed as digital forensic practitioners. Individuals who met this criterion were sent invitations requesting their participation. A total of 56 responses were received, which were then collated and analyzed. Based on the number of responses received, it is felt that the sample represented by the respondents is a fair representation of the total relevant population.

5.1 Questioning in Court About Tool Validation

When asked if they had ever been cross-examined in court about the validity of their forensic acquisition tool, only 7% of the sample stated that they had been asked if the tools they used were validated. However, none had been asked to provide proof of this by the lawyer leading the cross-examination. It must be pointed out that only 45% of the sample had ever testified in a court of law in their capacity as digital forensic practitioners.

It can be argued that digital forensic science has its intrinsic quality metric; namely, the evidence admitted into court and which stands up to vigorous cross-examination. Quality assurance can, however, increase the likelihood that the evidence and the processes applied to it can successfully stand up to this vigorous cross-examination. This is all good and well, but the key for this to be valid is that the digital forensic practitioners must testify and be subjected to vigorous cross-examination in court.

This is of significant concern, as these tools are a crucial component of preserving the digital evidence that is used in court. If the reliability of these tools is not challenged, there is a risk that digital evidence that should not be considered legally reliable may be relied upon in court, which could unfairly prejudice one side in the legal proceedings. In the experience of the researchers, in cases such as exceeding the speed limit when driving, or driving under the influence of alcohol, it is routine in court for the validity of the tools used to collect the evidence to be tested through cross-examination. Thus, it is concerning that the same principle is not being followed regarding the forensic acquisition of digital evidence.

It is, however, also concerning that while seven percent of the sample was questioned about the validity of their tools in court, none was asked to provide proof of this. In the experience of the researchers, where speed cameras and breathalyzers are used to obtain evidence for use in court, it is routine for the calibration certificates or other validation documents to be submitted to the court to prove that the results obtained were valid due to the tools working correctly. It concerns that the same is not done for digital evidence.

---

[1] https://www.linkedin.com.

5.2 Training About Tool Validation

Nine percent of the sample stated that they had received training on the importance of validation testing of the hardware and software used in the forensic acquisition process; however, only 2% of the sample stated that they had received training in how to conduct a validation test.

What is of significant concern is that only 2% had been formally trained to conduct validation testing.

5.3 Knowledge of Tool Validation Standards

The literature review identified three specific formal validation standards used in the field of digital forensics. The respondents were questioned to determine how they rated their knowledge of these standards. The responses are illustrated in Fig. 1.

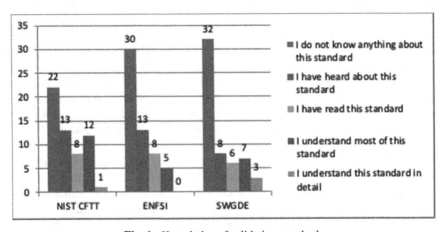

Fig. 1. Knowledge of validation standards

The graph suggests that most of the respondents are not able to apply these formal validation standards used in the field of digital forensics, as very few understand the various standards, either generally or in detail.

5.4 The Use and Validation of Write-Blockers

Twenty-five percent of the sample stated that they did not always use write blockers that had been validated as working correctly. The reasons given are illustrated in Fig. 2.

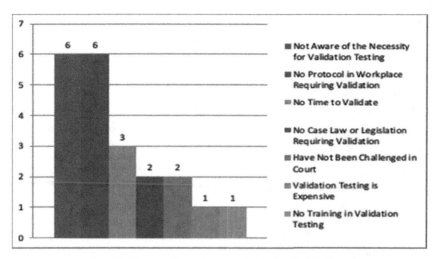

Fig. 2. Reasons for not using validated write blockers

Thirty-two percent of the sample claimed that they tested and validated the write blockers that they used. All were asked if they could produce copies of the documentation from their testing process, and all stated that they did not keep documentation, so it was not possible to verify if this had been done or not. To address the exact processes used, the researchers asked them to describe the testing processes that each used to validate the write blockers. All stated that they simply tried to copy a file onto media protected by a write blocker, and if the copy failed, the write blocker would be working. While there is some validity to this process, it does not meet the formal testing requirements of the validation testing standards discussed.

Forty-three percent of the sample stated that they only used validated write blockers, even though they did not test the write blockers themselves. The reasons provided by them for how they confirmed that the write blockers that they used were validated was due to the reasons in Fig. 3.

All the respondents were asked to provide documentation proving that the write blockers that they used had been validated and were unable to produce any documentation proving the validation.

The write blocking tools used by the members of the sample that stated that they used tools that were validated by the vendors, used the following tools: Tableau hardware write blocker, Wiebetech hardware write blocker, Deft, Caine, Fastblock SE, Voom, Paladin.

The websites of each tool were examined, and not a single website contained any references to a vendor validation documentation or testing. The end-user license agreements of all tools that had them were also examined, and all of them clearly stated that they provided no warranties as to the accuracy of their tools.

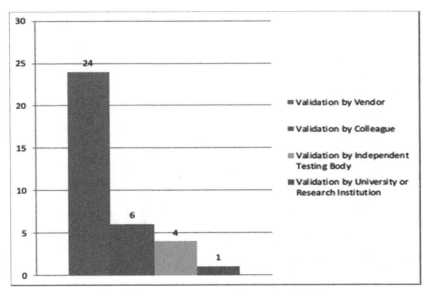

Fig. 3. How validation was done (write blocker)

5.5 The Use and Validation of Forensic Imaging Tools

Sixteen percent of the sample stated that they did not always use forensic imaging tools that had been validated as working correctly. The reasons given are illustrated in Fig. 4.

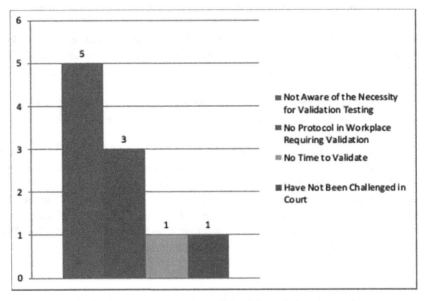

Fig. 4. Reasons for not using validated forensic imaging tools

Twenty-nine percent of the sample claimed that they tested and validated the forensic imaging tools that they used. All were asked if they could produce copies of the documentation from their testing process, and all stated that they did not keep documentation, so it was not possible to verify if this had been done or not. To identify the processes used, the researchers asked them to describe the testing processes that each used to validate the forensic imaging tools. Two primary methods were stated as having been used, dual tool validation using two different imaging tools to see if they got the same outcome and checking that the hash values after an image matched the hash values calculated of media before it was imaged. While there is some validity to these processes, they do not meet the formal testing requirements of the validation testing standards discussed.

Fifty-five percent of the sample stated that they only used validated forensic imaging tools, even though they did not test them themselves. The reasons provided by them for how they confirmed that the forensic imaging tools that they used were validated was due to the reasons in Fig. 5.

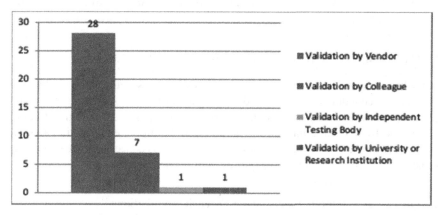

Fig. 5. Claimed proof of validation of forensic imagers

All the respondents were asked to provide documentation proving that the imaging tools that they used had been validated and were unable to produce any documentation proving the validation.

The imaging tools used by the members of the sample that stated that they used tools that were validated by the vendors, used the following tools:

- X-Ways Imager
- EnCase Imager
- FTK Imager
- Paladin
- dd (or other dd based command line variant)
- Hardware forensic imager

The websites of each tool were examined, and not a single website contained any references to a vendor validation documentation or testing. The end-user license agreements of all tools that had them were also examined, and all of them clearly stated that they provided no warranties as to the accuracy of their tools.

6 Conclusions

The review of the data provided by the sample showed significant concerns with regards to the validation of hardware and software tools used in the acquisition of digital evidence. Mainly three categories could be identified.

- Category One – Digital forensic practitioners that did not make use of validated tools
- Category Two – Digital forensic practitioners that believed the tools that they used were validated by another party
- Category Three – Digital forensic practitioners that claimed to have tested the tools they used themselves.

6.1 The Use of Non-validated Tools During Forensic Acquisitions

Twenty-five percent of the sample stated that they did not use validated write blockers, and sixteen percent did not use validated imaging tools. This is even though the requirement to use validated write blockers is a foundational requirement of digital forensics practice, and by not doing this, have compromised the digital evidence in cases they have done. Even though this lack of using validated tools is concerning, the honesty and openness from this portion of the sample are commended.

6.2 The Use of Validated Tools During Forensic Acquisitions

Seventy-five percent of the sample stated that they used validated write blockers, and eighty-four percent used validated imaging tools. The most significant concern with the members of the sample that claimed that they always used validated tools, was that not even one of them was able to produce any form of documentation verifying their claims that the tools that they were used had been validated. There was thus no way to assess the veracity of their claims objectively. A cornerstone of digital forensics practice is to be able to back up everything that the digital forensic practitioner states, with evidence, and being unable to provide any evidence shows either a dangerous departure from accepted digital forensics practice at best or at worst deliberate deception whereby claims are made that validated tools are used when that is not the case.

6.3 Self-validation of Tools

Thirty-two percent of the sample claimed that they tested their write blockers, and twenty-nine percent stated they are testing their imaging tools. The various methods that they stated they used, while not meeting the full requirements of validation testing as set out in the respective validation standards, would at least provide a certain level of confidence in the tools used. However, the fact that no-one was able to produce any documentation verifying that these tests had taken place meant that this could not be objectively proven.

6.4 Vendor "Validation"

One area of significant concern was the statement that fifty percent of the sample believed they write blocking tools they used, and forty-three percent of the sample believed that their imaging tools were validated by the vendors of those tools.

However, none of these tools had any available vendor validation documentation available on their websites, and the End User License Agreements also provided no warranties as to the accuracy of the various tools. Legally the providers of these tools have conclusively stated that their tools were used "as is" and, as such, are effectively stating that they are not validating these tools. If South African digital forensic practitioners are relying on a belief that vendor tools are validated by the vendors, then this belief is ill-informed.

6.5 The Impact on the Reliability of Digital Evidence

Section 15 of the Electronic Communications and Transactions Act 25 of 2002 deals with the admissibility and weight of digital evidence in South Africa. Section 15(1) of the Act states that digital evidence cannot be ruled inadmissible only by the evidence being in an intangible digital format, while Sect. 15(2) goes on to state that information in a digital form must be given due evidential weight [1].

Section 15(3) lays down the issues that a court must consider in assessing the evidential weight of the digital evidence, and requires a court to do so:

- Consider the reliability of the way the digital evidence was generated, stored, or communicated.
- Consider the reliability of the way the integrity of the digital evidence was maintained.
- Consider the way the originator of the digital evidence was established.
- Consider any other relevant factors.

The lack of actual validation of forensic tools, or evidence of validation, can have a significant impact on the reliability of digital evidence in a court of law. This means that digital evidence, which is preserved through the use of specific hardware or software tools and is then presented and relied upon as evidence in a court of law, is preserved by tools where the objective and scientific validity thereof cannot be determined. Considering that South African courts must take into consideration reliability in terms of Sect. 15(3) of the Electronic Communications and Transactions Act 25 of 2002 in assessing the weight of digital evidence, the weight of digital evidence is undermined through the current state of practice in South Africa by digital forensic practitioners.

6.6 Failure of the Justice System

Based on an examination of the data, it is suggested that testifying in court is not currently an effective method for determining if write blockers or forensic imaging tools have been validated. The researchers believe that digital forensic practitioners have so far managed to get away with these practices because, so few have testified in court (only 45% of the sample), and even fewer have been questioned about the tools they used (only 7% of the sample). The reasons for this have not been established, but the contributing factor for this may be the relative infancy of the use of digital evidence in South Africa court proceedings, as well as digital forensics. When one looks at established forensic sciences such as forensic toxicology, the validation and calibration of the instruments used in the forensic examination are regularly tested in court, and the validity and reliability thereof established through formal validation or calibration documents.

7 Future Research

The first area of suggested research is the effectiveness of current digital forensics training and education in South Africa, especially in equipping digital forensic practitioners with the core technical and scientific skills required in the field of digital forensics, such as validation testing.

The second area of suggested research is the lack of understanding of digital forensics processes and procedures within the legal community, due in part to the limited number of instances where digital forensic practitioners have been cross-examined and questioned about the validity of the tools they use. If legal practitioners were more knowledgeable of digital forensics, would they not be more vigilant in how they address digital evidence in court regarding its admissibility and reliability?

References

1. Republic of South Africa. Electronic Communications and Transactions Act 25 of 2002. South Africa (2002)
2. Marcella, A.J., Guillossou, F.: Cyber Forensics. Wiley, Hoboken (2012)
3. Casey, E., Rose, C.W.: Forensic analysis. In: Casey, E. (ed.) Handbook of Digital Forensics and Investigation, pp. 21–62. Academic Press, London (2010)
4. Guo, Y., Slay, J., Beckett, J.: Validation and verification of computer forensic software tools—searching Function. Digit. Investig. Int. J. Digit. Forensics Incid. Response6, S12–S22 (2009)
5. Jordaan, J.: A sample of digital forensic quality assurance in the South African criminal justice system. In: 2012 Information Security for South Africa - Proceedings of the ISSA 2012 Conference (2012). https://doi.org/10.1109/ISSA.2012.6320431.
6. Nelson, B., Phillips, A., Enfinger, F., Steuart, C.: Guide to Computer Forensics and Investigations, 3rd edn. Course Technology, Boston (2008)
7. Association of Chief Police Officers. Good Practice Guide for Computer-Based Electronic Evidence, London (2003)
8. Sansurooah, K.: Taxonomy of computer forensics methodologies and procedures for digital evidence seizure. In: Australian Digital Forensics Conference, p. 32 (2006)
9. Casey, E.: "What does" forensically sound "really mean? "Digit. Investig. Int. J. Digit. Forensics Incid. Response4(2), 49–50 (2007)

10. National Institute of Justice (US). Technical Working Group for Electronic Crime Scene, Electronic crime scene investigation: A guide for first responders. US Department of Justice, Office of Justice Programs, National Institute of … (2001)
11. Barbara, J.J.: Quality assurance practices for computer forensics part 1. Forensic Mag. (2007)
12. Casey, E.: Digital Evidence and Computer Crime: Forensic Science, Computers, and the Internet. Academic Press, London (2011)
13. National Research Council, Discussion of the Committee on Daubert Standards: Summary of Meetings. National Academies Press (2006)
14. Wilsdon, T., Slay, J.: Validation of forensic computing software utilizing Black Box testing techniques. In: Australian Digital Forensics Conference, p. 37 (2006)
15. Carrier, B.: Defining digital forensic examination and analysis tools using abstraction layers. Int. J. Digit. Evid. 1(4), 1–2 (2003)
16. Pan, L., Batten, L.M.: Robust performance testing for digital forensic tools. Digit. Investig. 6(1–2), 71–81 (2009)
17. Scientific Working Group on Digital Evidence, "SWGDE Recommended Guidelines for Validation Testing," Washington DC (2009)
18. European Network of Forensic Science Institutes, "Guidelines for Best Practice in the Forensic Examination of Digital Technology," The Hague (2009)
19. Meyers, M., Rogers, M.: Digital forensics: meeting the challenges of scientific evidence. In: IFIP International Conference on Digital Forensics, pp. 43–50 (2005)
20. Saunders, M., Lewis, P., Thornhill, A.: Research Methods for Business Students, 5th edn. Prentice Hall, Harlow (2009)

Investigating Customer-Facing Security Features on South African E-commerce Websites

Deen Brandreth[1] and Jacques Ophoff[1,2(✉)] (iD)

[1] University of Cape Town, Cape Town, South Africa
deen.brandreth@uct.ac.za, j.ophoff@abertay.ac.uk
[2] Abertay University, Dundee, UK

Abstract. E-commerce websites often store sensitive customer information and there is the impression that customers are not as concerned about protecting their data as they should be. Instead they often choose convenience over security. There are those who argue that e-vendors do not provide the necessary environment to adequately protect their customers' data by utilizing multi-factor authentication and by providing customer support that educates and encourages customers to follow security best practices. This study develops criteria to evaluate website security and goes on to investigate how the top 20 South African e-commerce websites perform against this. The results show that multi-factor authentication is underutilized and security in the form of password-based authentication can be improved. Furthermore, despite many customer support channels and resources, there is little emphasis placed on educating and encouraging customers to follow security best practices. The results suggest areas for security improvement in order to build trust in e-commerce websites.

Keywords: E-commerce · Security features · Account creation · Login · Security management

1 Introduction

Despite its growth, e-commerce is still relatively new to many people [1]. An e-commerce customer tends to accept far more risk during a transaction than a traditional offline customer [2]. There are those who believe that e-commerce has yet to reach its full potential and one of the major factors impeding this is a lack of trust between the customer, the system facilitating the transaction and the e-commerce business [2–4].

For a website to be considered secure data should be transmitted securely between the customer and the website. Customer data stored on the website should also be stored in a secure manner so that only authorized entities have access to it [5]. These two categories can be called transactional data and customer information. A typical solution for securing transactional data would be encryption while customer information is often protected using authentication and verification [5, 6].

Customers' perception of security is one of the biggest factors that determine whether they will transact online [3, 6–8]. This perception of security lies in the risk of sensitive

© Springer Nature Switzerland AG 2020
H. Venter et al. (Eds.): ISSA 2020, CCIS 1339, pp. 144–159, 2020.
https://doi.org/10.1007/978-3-030-66039-0_10

personal and payment information being compromised [6, 7]. Regular and consistent security reviews with the implementation of solutions is thus a prerequisite to success in e-commerce [9].

Based on security literature, this paper proposes criteria for evaluating the level of security that an e-commerce website provides customers. Instead of a purely technical analysis of security features the criteria consider a broader range of issues and aims to give a typical customer several indicators of trust for the e-vendor. The criteria are separated into three phases which include account creation, login, and security management.

A sample consisting of the top 20 South African e-commerce websites is then evaluated against the criteria, to determine the perception of security and trust a customer may have of the website. Purchase of goods or services is specifically excluded from the evaluation, as security during this process is more standardized (e.g. PCI-DSS) and technical features may be less visible to the customer.

The remainder of this paper proceeds as follows. Section 2 provides a background discussion leading to the proposed criteria. Next, Sect. 3 reviews the research methodology and how the sample was selected. This is followed by analysis and a discussion of the findings in Sect. 4, after which the paper concludes with a brief summary.

2   Background

E-commerce plays a pivotal role in the global economy and particularly in developing countries, where there is a growing middle class and companies from around the world serving the need for better quality and more convenient shopping [2]. The significant growth of e-commerce can partly be attributed to the fact that the internet has become ingrained in our daily lives [3]. However, given the rise in targeted phishing and other social engineering attacks [10], data security should be a primary concern for both e-commerce businesses and the customers who use their platforms.

A customer, a vendor, one or more third parties such as certification authorities or payment systems and the technological system facilitating the trade, are the various actors in an e-commerce transaction and since the customer decides whether or not to transact, you could consider them to be the most important of the four [3]. Trust needs to be established between these actors but of utmost importance is the level of trust experienced by the customer [3, 6]. The customer should, therefore, believe that the e-vendor will act in their best interest during and after the transaction or exchange. To define trust is not easy as there are many considerations of which context is very important. Trust has been studied in the context of psychology, economics, sociology and management studies but for the purpose of this paper, trust will be defined simply as "a belief that one party (the trustee) will behave in a manner which is in the interest of another party (the trustor), through transactions or exchanges" [2].

2.1   Increasing Customer Trust

Some researchers argue that trust cannot exist without doubt [3]. It stands to reason then, that the factors that increase risk and doubt in an online environment must be dealt with before trust can be established. In a traditional context, the customer may have the opportunity to observe the vendor in person through a handshake or reading body language [6] but in an online context, this is not possible.

Oliveira et al. [1] point to three properties of trust, namely "competence, integrity and benevolence". These are said to be established by the character of both the customer and the e-vendor and by the website functionality. McCole et al. [3] also include properties of compassion, aptitude and certainty along with those mentioned by Oliveira et al., but do not consider the website and its functionality as needing trust. Instead, they consider that trust in the entire system that facilitates the transaction along with the e-vendor and other third parties involved in the transaction is required.

Steyn and Mawela [2] have found that trust is formed based on the customer's own core beliefs of what is normal and acceptable, technological aspects and due to experiences with the e-vendor and system over a period. They have also identified further categories such as cognitive, institutional, calculative, knowledge based and reputational trust where trust is based on factors that fall under these descriptions. For example, cognition-based trust occurs when the customer considers aspects such as privacy and security or the quality of the system, they are interacting with whereas institutional trust speaks to aspects of laws, regulations and third-party guarantees and certification [2]. Thus, it stands to reason that for a customer to trust an e-vendor or their website, some of the important considerations lie around privacy, security, quality of the user interface, website functionality and the use of trusted third parties. As such, these concepts, as they relate to e-commerce websites, were considered as key factors in this study.

2.2 Privacy in E-Commerce

Privacy in e-commerce refers to the right of customers and organizations to have control over how their personal data is stored and transmitted to others [4, 11, 12]. Privacy is a growing concern, specifically for customers who transact online in fear of their information being used fraudulently [7, 8]. Customer privacy is not new or specific to e-commerce but in order to thrive, e-vendors do have to provide assurance that customer data is secure. Chatterjee [8] argues that privacy and security issues can determine whether a business succeeds or fails. These privacy fears are further fueled because of aggressive data collection by both public and private sector organizations with some companies using collected data for marketing and monitoring purposes [4]. As such, many e-vendors include privacy policies on their websites to remove customers' fears about how their information is managed [11]. Privacy policies are an indication to the customer that the e-vendor is concerned about privacy [4] which should positively influence trust in the e-vendor [11].

Regardless of privacy policies and assurance about how data is managed, caution should still be exercised when transacting online. Customers are encouraged to only share information that is required and only use secure websites that utilize encryption [4, 8].

2.3 Security from a Customer's Perspective

Customers may have sensitive financial and health data stored/exchanged with e-commerce servers or accounts, which makes security even more imperative [13]. When it comes to securing online accounts, authentication is the primary means of doing so [14].

Passwords are the most common means of end user authentication to protect data on computer systems. At an early stage in the evolution of computer security the end user was identified as a major weakness in the use of passwords as a means of authentication [15]. Many years later research still identifies the end user as a weak link in password-based authentication systems, e.g. "password-based authentication is frequently criticized on the basis of the ways in which the approach can be compromised by end users" [16]. Furnell et al. [17] go so far as to call the end user "the weakest link in the information security realm". The end user, unfortunately, is not the only weakness to be exploited when it comes to password-based authentication systems. Technically incorrect or insufficient security implementations can be equally problematic.

Researchers have found numerous ways of mitigating the potential exploitation of these weaknesses. Some suggest adding additional layers of authentication, known as multi-factor authentication [18–21] while others point out that supporting the end user by providing information and feedback to increase security awareness, is another means of improving the success of password-based authentication systems [17, 22].

Supporting the user is typically done in an active or passive manner. Passive support simply provides information and advice to aid the user in making better security related decisions. This could take the form of a frequently asked questions webpage, games, educational programs and self-assessment checklists [17]. Although effective in bringing about change in user actions and attitude, passive support is not resolving the issue in its entirety and so active intervention is gaining popularity. This would include a more direct approach of coaxing users to comply with security policies through interactive feedback such as highlighting poor choices and things like password meters [17].

2.4 Security Evaluation Criteria

There is little research documenting the extent of multi-factor authentication or how end-users are supported and guided by those who have implemented it. Studies around password practice and user support have shown that there are tangible benefits to providing support and guidance to end-users, with the aim of improving the security and protection of user accounts and data. It therefore makes sense that e-vendors who offer online accounts should provide support with the aim of educating their customers in order to mitigate the likelihood of unauthorized access to customer data. It is agreed that there is no silver bullet to resolve these issues but using a layered approach to security is certainly better than not doing anything at all.

The key concepts identified in the literature review were privacy, security, website functionality, and the use of trusted third parties. These were then considered when designing the criteria in the *Website Security Analysis Criteria*, as shown in Table 1.

The criteria consider three distinct phases of security analysis, namely account creation/registration, the login process, and after gaining access to the site as a registered

Table 1. Website security analysis criteria

Criteria	Account creation	Login	Security management
Security			
Does the site use HTTPS? (Is the connection secure?)	X	X	
Is the HTTPS certificate valid?	X		
What are the password requirements (if any)?	X		
Does the account get locked after entering the incorrect password?		X	
Is there a forgot password option? /Is there an option to change the password?		X	X
How is the password reset, i.e. use of account recovery questions, new password auto-generated, link provided to change password, or OTP sent?		X	
What are the communication options when resetting pin, i.e. email, SMS, app, etc.?		X	
What are the password requirements when changing passwords?		X	X
Is multi-factor authentication offered?	X	X	
What multi-factor authentication settings are available?			X
What other settings are available for securing the account?			X
Are you required to verify any information, e.g. email address? (How is this done?)	X		
Does the website allow for third-party login?	X	X	
Privacy			
What personal information is required to sign up?	X		
What additional personal information is requested (but not compulsory) when signing up?	X		
What additional personal information can be added in account settings?			X

(*continued*)

Table 1. (*continued*)

Criteria	Account creation	Login	Security management
Support/Awareness			
Are there any security prompts, e.g. password strength indicators?	X		
Are security indicators explained in more detail or are there links for additional information?	X		X
What are the various types of help resources available?	X	X	X
Does the site have a privacy policy?	X		X
Is there a link to terms and conditions?	X		

user while browsing the site for available account settings and support resources (security management). In each phase the focus is on information which would be visible to the customer. While additional technical criteria (such as HTTPS certificate issuer, cryptographic settings, etc.) could be considered important, the criteria is aimed at non-technical users and information readily obtained on a website. Criteria to consider are separated into security, privacy, and support or awareness issues. The applicability of each criteria within the three phases is indicated with an *"X"*.

The next section explains how the criteria was used to evaluate actual security settings on a relevant sample of e-commerce websites.

3 Methodology

This study used documentary secondary data in the form security-related settings, text, and video found in the help sections of the various e-commerce websites, as well as potential external sources that the websites refer customers to. Settings related to multi-factor authentication and account security in general were also noted for analysis. Data was reduced into content categories before being analyzed qualitatively. Referred to as content analysis, this technique aims to "quantify and describe aspects of textual or visual data after coding and categorizing them" [23]. Content analysis is based on objective observation of factual objects and analyzing what is clear and obvious, as opposed to interpreting the data subjectively.

3.1 Sampling

A well-known longitudinal study used ten popular websites, as ranked by Alexa (https://www.alexa.com/topsites), to identify how these websites managed password security [16, 20]. Similarly, this study uses the Alexa ranking system to identify the top 20 South African e-commerce websites. The rankings are calculated using a combination of average daily visitors and pageviews. The sample was determined using website traffic at a specific point in time: in this case the top 500 websites were retrieved in July 2019. A set of selection criteria were applied to identify the final list of e-commerce websites, which included:

- The website is used to conduct business.
- The website facilitates transactions for the sale of goods or services. Some online marketplaces or classifieds allow free advertising and viewing of adverts. In this manner, an entire transaction is free of charge and the website was disqualified.
- The website requires an account to be created in order to transact. Websites that allow free viewing of adverts but required an account and payment to advertise was included.

Company details were confirmed on the appropriate domain registration authority's website. It was also confirmed that the company is registered in South Africa by searching the Companies and Intellectual Properties Commission website. The final list of included websites is shown in Table 2. The table shows the e-commerce rank, website URL, as well as overall country (South African) ranking.

Table 2. Websites selected for analysis

Rank	Website	Overall	Rank	Website	Overall
1	Takealot.com	9	2	Property24.com	19
3	Hollywoodbets.net	34	4	Showmax.co.za	46
5	Bidorbuy.co.za	52	6	Privateproperty.co.za	68
7	Makro.co.za	73	8	Sageone.co.za	92
9	Afrihost.com	101	10	Vodacom.co.za	104
11	Builders.co.za	136	12	Nationallottery.co.za	137
13	Superbalist.com	149	14	Loot.co.za	155
15	Evetech.co.za	159	16	Game.co.za	167
17	Onedayonly.co.za	179	18	Clicks.co.za	184
19	Zando.co.za	188	20	Altcointrader.co.za	197

Since the rankings are based on site traffic, it can be said that these are the most frequented South African e-commerce websites as visited by South Africans. This does not imply that these are the most successful e-commerce websites or that they have the most online accounts, but it does allow the researcher to comply with the principles of scientific research in that it contributes to making the study replicable.

3.2 Data Collection

The data was collected by assuming the role of a customer. An account was created on each of the websites using an email account created specifically for this study. This process was documented using the Website Security Analysis Criteria (Table 1) as a guide, screen captures, notes about the experience (sequence of processes, type and timing of communications), information such as security prompts and restrictions that are applied (restrictions related to enforcement of security features such as multi-factor authentication and password strength, etc.), built-in tools that assist and advise the customer, links to help/support resources (including the data they contain whether in the form of text, audio or video) and all other available security options.

After the initial account creation, all security options, related to the account, were documented in the same way that the account creation process was documented. Here the researcher looked for replication of settings, additional options and settings that were not presented during the account creation process and whether password requirements were enforced or if they differed from the account creation stage. This was followed by collecting data on all the support options related to security. These took the form of help sections with knowledge base articles, frequently asked questions (FAQ) pages, documentation related to multi-factor authentication and account security, video and other interactive help tools. Data pertaining to support provided on the actual website and support that is provided offsite, for which links are provided, was also collected.

4 Analysis and Discussion

Analysis focused on three stages: account creation/registration, the login process, and after gaining access to the site as a registered user by observing available account security settings. The first step in data analysis was to clean up and sort the data because different websites use different terms to describe the same data. For example, one website would use the term surname where a different website would request your last name when registering an account. Similarly, some sites had a password reset feature, while others would refer to this as a forgot password option. Similar terms were renamed to standardize the terminology used. Settings were grouped into the following categories:

- Security

  - Account security: Multi factor authentication, password requirements, account lockout for entering the incorrect password, are the password requirements enforced and other account security settings.
  - Website security: Use of HTTPS, validity of certificate, and a secure connection between the customer device and website.

- Privacy

  - Types of information stored as part of the account. These include personally identifiable information such as first name, last name, identity number, passport number or contact information such as the mobile number and email address.
  - The use of privacy policies and/or terms and conditions.

- Customer support options (considered to be a function of the website)

  - Any method of contact between the e-vendor and the customer which allows the e-vendor to provide support information through direct communication (email, telephone, etc.) and indirect communication (videos, social media posts, help articles, FAQs, interactive website features, etc.).

- The use of third parties

  - Allowing third-party login, for example using Facebook, Google, Microsoft, etc.
  - Using a third-party to facilitate security. An example would be Takealot.com and OneDayOnly.co.za who use GoDaddy.com to facilitate site security and their payment system.

4.1 Privacy

Given the diverse offering of services and products, it stands to reason that there is a similarly diverse range of information stored on these platforms, making them a potential target for cyber criminals. It is no surprise that the most common information required on these websites are first name, last name, email address and mobile number. What is surprising is that half of these websites potentially store customers' ID numbers while about a third store home phone numbers, work phone numbers and physical addresses of customers. Potentially sensitive data includes: Mobile/Home/Work Phone Number; Date of Birth; ID/Passport Number; Physical/Postal Address; Credit Card Details; Bank Account Number; Type of Income; E-vendor Account Number; FICA Documents (ID and Proof of Address).

All but one of the sites have a privacy policy. The privacy policy explains how e-vendors manage customers' information. Privacy policies detail, to the customer, which personal information is collected, how the data is processed, who the data is shared with and also lists the type of information collected that the customer may not be aware of such as IP addresses, browsing data, location information, website preferences, operating system information and all electronic communications between e-vendor and customer. Another common theme, found within the privacy policies, is the assurance that the e-vendors try and convey to their customers that their data is safe, that the e-vendor is compliant from a legal perspective, that their systems are safe and of course that they have the customers' best interest at heart, e.g. *"we are committed to protecting and respecting your privacy"*.

4.2 Account Security

All the websites, except one, use password-based authentication to restrict access to customer accounts. This is in line with many researchers who point out that password-based authentication is still the most widely used form of authentication despite the many known weaknesses. The odd one out is Nationallottery.co.za which only requires a five-digit pin in conjunction with the customer's mobile number for authentication.

Since most of the e-vendors opt to use password-based authentication systems, it is interesting to note how many of them configure their systems in a way that would mitigate the many pitfalls associated with passwords. Unfortunately, only half of the websites investigated require a complex password consisting of a mix of upper- and lower-case letters, numbers and special characters. The other half allow the creation of simple passwords by only requiring a minimum amount of characters. In all cases where only the minimum number of characters were specified as a requirement, the researcher could create a password of a string of consecutive numbers such as *"123456"* for example. One of the websites, however, did not even enforce the minimum requirements of five characters. Once an account was registered, the researcher was able to change the password to a single digit on Evetech.co.za, log out and log back in with the password *"1"*.

The next examined setting was account lockout for incorrect password attempts. The researcher made 20 incorrect attempts before trying the correct password if no prompts were received. Again, the results were not positive. Only four out of the ten websites that allow simple passwords, locked the account after several unsuccessful login attempts. In total, seven websites utilized this security measure. Table 3 describes the minimum password requirements and the account lockout security feature for each website.

Only two of the websites have opted to use multi-factor authentication for securing their customers' accounts. Altcointrader.co.za have made multi-factor authentication, using Google's Authenticator app, optional on their site. Afrihost has taken the decision out of their customer's hands and appear to re-quire a one-time pin (OTP) for login at their own discretion. This notably caused some concern as the feature took customers by surprise when first introduced, as can be seen by a post on the Afrihost forum [24]:

"I received the following notice from Afrihost: 'An OTP has been requested on your Afrihost Account' What is an OTP?" asked Nov 26, 2018 in General by Swart (190 points)

The answer to which was: *"An OTP is a one time pin - they sometimes send you one when you try to access your account to make sure that no one has stolen your login details" answered Dec 5, 2018 by FearsomePiratePete (180 points)*

Some customers were clearly not informed about the introduction of multi-factor authentication or missed the communication. Other customers were unable to access their accounts as they could not receive the OTP for various reasons. One such post on the forum reads [25]:

"Look, this is an obvious question and one that affects me greatly (and inconvenient also !!) is that ibn [sic] my area my Vodacom signal is frequently down or too weak to even carry a bar for SMS delivery. How can Afrihost be so careless of clients needs as to introduce a silly SMS verification system for login to Client Zone??" asked Mar 20, 2019 in Client Zone by GarethG (120 points)

4.3 Website Security

The use of a secure, encrypted connection between customer and e-vendor was found to be standard practice on all the top 20 South African e-commerce websites and all website certificates were valid. Hollywoodbets.net was the anomaly in this case though. Although their website is secure, uploading of FICA documents is not done over a

Table 3. Website account security

Site	Password requirements	Account lockout
Takealot.com	Minimum 5 characters	Yes. Warning after 7th incorrect attempt that there are 3 attempts left
Property24.com	Minimum 6 characters. Password must have both upper- and lower-case letters and a symbol or number	No. 20 incorrect attempts and then successful login with correct password
Hollywoodbets.net	Minimum 4 characters	Unable to log in as I have not submitted FICA documents
Showmax.com	Minimum 6 characters	No. 20 incorrect attempts and then successful login with the correct password
Bidorbuy.co.za	Minimum 8 characters, minimum 1 upper case letter and minimum 1 number	No. 20 incorrect attempts and then successful login with correct password
Privateproperty.co.za	6–50 characters	No. 20 incorrect attempts and then successful login with correct password
Makro.co.za	8–32 characters, no spaces, must have upper- and lower-case letter, must have at least 1 number	Yes. Correct password did not work after 20 incorrect attempts. Had to reset password before gaining access to account
Sageone.co.za	Minimum 6 characters, 1 lower case letter, 1 upper case letter, 1 number, 1 special character	No. 20 incorrect attempts and then successful login with correct password
Afrihost.com	Minimum 6 characters. Could use 5 characters in password once registered	Yes. Had to reset password after 20 incorrect attempts. The account becomes active after 5 min
Vodacom.co.za	Minimum 8 characters, 1 number, 1 upper case and 1 lower case letter. Password reset from profile doesn't require old password	Yes. Have to reset password after 3 incorrect attempts. OTP sent to email to allow password reset
Builders.co.za	Minimum 6 characters, 1 upper and 1 lower case letter and 1 number and no spaces	No. 20 incorrect attempts and then successful login with correct password
Nationallottery.co.za	5-digit pin	No. 20 incorrect attempts and then successful login with correct pin

(continued)

Table 3. (*continued*)

Site	Password requirements	Account lockout
Superbalist.co.za	Minimum 6 characters	No. 20 incorrect attempts and then successful login with correct password
Loot.co.za	Minimum 6 characters	No. 20 incorrect attempts and then successful login with correct password
Evetech.co.za	Minimum 5 characters at account creation but single digit password accepted after registration	No. 20 incorrect attempts and then successful login with correct password
Game.co.za	Minimum 6 characters	Yes. Correct password did not work after 20 incorrect attempts. Had to reset password before gaining access to account
Onedayonly.co.za	Minimum 6 characters	No. 20 incorrect attempts and then successful login with correct password.
Clicks.co.za	Minimum 6 characters	Yes. Correct password did not work after 20 incorrect attempts. Had to reset password before gaining access to account
Zando.co.za	Minimum 6 characters	No. 20 incorrect attempts and then successful login with correct password
Altcointrader.co.za	Minimum 8 characters, at least 1 letter and at 1 number and a 24-h hold is placed on withdrawals when password is changed	Yes. Account blocked after 3 failed attempts. Blocked for 30 min

secure connection when following links via their website support section. However, when viewing a how-to video the URL indicated in the video did display as HTTPS and when navigating to it the upload could be done securely.

Third-Party Login. Third-party logins are allowed on seven of the 20 websites. These were restricted to Google and Facebook. Both Facebook and Google have the option of using multi-factor authentication for enhanced account security.

Furthermore, most of the websites actively advertise secure payments. These are provided by third parties such as PayU, MasterCard, Visa, GoDaddy, Thawte and MyGate. Sageone.co.za are the only e-vendor who have their own payment gateway. Showmax is one of the few sites who don't actively advertise transaction security, but they do offer an extensive range of payment options. These include PayPal, the option to add the subscription to one of several other subscriptions such as DSTV, Telkom, Vodacom, MTN and by purchasing vouchers from third parties.

Support. There is a myriad of support resources that e-vendors can use to interact with and provide support to their customers. Social media is the most utilized means of communicating with customers as all the studied e-vendors make use of YouTube and Facebook while 19 have a Twitter account. A dedicated FAQ section follows as the most popular means of providing support with a total of 17 websites utilizing this support resource. Telephone contact is also supplied for 19 websites but not all of them indicate this as a means of support. Other electronic forms of support such as blogs and email are also well utilized. Forums and live chat, which are a more immediate forms of support are only used by five and four of the e-vendors respectively. It is no surprise that fewer e-vendors provide a physical address as a means of contact. Of the eight websites that provide this type of detail, five are major retailers with stores countrywide.

As mentioned above, social media is used extensively to provide support. Table 4 lists the number of videos that the e-vendors have uploaded to their official YouTube channels. The researcher could only find eight videos which mentioned security or privacy.

Table 4. Videos per e-Vendor

Site	Total YouTube Videos	Account security/privacy videos
Takealot.com	73	0
Property24.com	64	0
Hollywoodbets.net	223	2
Showmax.com	857	0
Bidorbuy.co.za	50	0
Privateproperty.co.za	51 316	0
Makro.co.za	107	0
Sageone.co.za	43	1
Afrihost.com	20	2
Vodacom.co.za	1 471	1
Builders.co.za	743	0
Nationallottery.co.za	933	0
Superbalist.co.za	117	0
Loot.co.za	4	0
Evetech.co.za	265	0
Game.co.za	182	0
Onedayonly.co.za	14	0
Clicks.co.za	369	0
Zando.co.za	115	2
Altcointrader.co.za	27	0

A total of 25 different types of support resources were counted (social media not counted as a collective). Afrihost.com provide the largest number of support resources with six other e-vendors providing ten or more. The rest of the websites provide six to nine options for support. Active support in the form of password strength meters and other interactive functionality is lacking. Only eight of the 20 websites provide feedback to users while they enter their password.

4.4 Discussion

There is a considerable variety of data stored on e-commerce platforms. Some of the data can be considered more sensitive than others especially if accessed by criminals. Some data such as first and last names can be considered less critical than other pieces of information such as ID or passport numbers or contact information such as home and mobile phone numbers. Customers who register on e-commerce websites should ideally store as little information as possible and only divulge information of a more critical nature if absolutely required. The nature of some e-commerce sites requires their customers to submit sensitive information in which case it is the responsibility of the e-vendor to ensure that the information is stored and transmitted safely and securely. Privacy policies indicate how the e-vendor intends managing the customers' information. All the websites investigated, except for one, have done so adequately thereby hopefully increasing the level of trust experienced by their customers.

The next step would be to follow through and provide a safe environment for customer's information. Somehow more emphasis is placed on transactional data security using encryption and third-party payment providers compared to the more basic approach applied to the protection of customer data stored in their accounts. Cost is certainly a consideration when e-vendors decide how to configure authentication on their websites and so is usability of the website. If cost were the only consideration, then one would expect the e-vendors to require more complex passwords or make more use of the account lockout feature as a means of re-enforcing account security. The researcher would argue that ease of use and convenience for the customer carries more weight than information security.

The lack of support aimed at educating and encouraging the customer from a security perspective also indicates that more can be done by the e-vendor to improve the protection of customer information. This is evident by comparing the amount of support that covers areas such as product support and advertising/marketing to the amount of content covering account security. One of the key support features were the forums of Bidorbuy.co.za and Afrihost.com. These forums provided an interactive platform where security was a hot topic and questions could be answered conveniently and in detail. Community powered support resources is an avenue that more e-vendors should utilize.

5   Conclusion

Security should be a primary concern for all e-vendors regardless of the size or nature of their business. Given the importance that cyber criminals place on data, customer information should be protected adequately. It was established that the top 20 South

African e-commerce websites generally take a very basic approach to account security. Multi-factor authentication is said to improve account security by adding one or more additional steps to the authentication process. Only two of the websites investigated made use of this security feature. It was further established that many of the websites do not provide an environment within which customers can empower themselves. Many of the websites appear to favor convenience over security. There is a clear lack of education and encouragement within customer support resources. Emphasis is placed on providing support related to products and services with only a fraction of effort aimed towards account security. There is room for improvement in terms of how e-vendors configure authentication and the type and volume of support provided to address customer account security.

References

1. Oliveira, T., Alhinho, M., Rita, P., Dhillon, G.: Modelling and testing consumer trust dimensions in e-commerce. Comput. Hum. Behav. **71**, 153–164 (2017). https://doi.org/10.1016/j.chb.2017.01.050
2. Steyn, L.J., Mawela, T.: A trust-based e-commerce decision-making model for South African Citizens. In: Proceedings of the Annual Conference of the South African Institute of Computer Scientists and Information Technologists, pp. 42:1–42:9. ACM, New York, (2016). https://doi.org/10.1145/2987491.2987496
3. McCole, P., Ramsey, E., Williams, J.: Trust considerations on attitudes towards online purchasing: The moderating effect of privacy and security concerns. J. Bus. Res. **63**(9), 1018–1024 (2010). https://doi.org/10.1016/j.jbusres.2009.02.025
4. Udo, G.: Privacy and security concerns as major barriers for e-commerce: a survey study. Inf. Manag. Comput. Secur. **9**(4), 165–174 (2001). https://doi.org/10.1108/EUM0000000005808
5. Mahadevan, L., Kaleta, J.P.: Consumer perceptions about E-commerce- the influence of public internet trust. In: Southern Association for Information Systems Conference 2017. St. Simons Island (2017). http://aisel.aisnet.org/sais2017
6. Kim, M.-J., Chung, N., Lee, C.-K.: The effect of perceived trust on electronic commerce: shopping online for tourism products and services in South Korea. Tourism Manage. **32**(2), 256–265 (2011). https://doi.org/10.1016/j.tourman.2010.01.011
7. Chang, H.H., Chen, S.W.: Consumer perception of interface quality, security, and loyalty in electronic commerce. Inf. Manag. **46**(7), 411–417 (2009). https://doi.org/10.1016/j.im.2009.08.002
8. Chatterjee, S.: Security and privacy issues in E-Commerce: a proposed guidelines to mitigate the risk. In: 2015 IEEE International Advance Computing Conference (IACC), pp. 393–396 (2015). https://doi.org/10.1109/IADCC.2015.7154737
9. Ladan, M.I.: E-Commerce security issues. In: 2014 International Conference on Future Internet of Things and Cloud, pp. 197–201 (2014). https://doi.org/10.1109/FiCloud.2014.39
10. Proofpoint. PROTECTING PEOPLE: A Quarterly Analysis of Highly Targeted Cyber Attacks (2018). https://www.proofpoint.com/sites/default/files/gtd-pfpt-us-tr-protecting-people-autumn-2018.pdf
11. Chen, Y.-H., Hsu, I.-C., Lin, C.-C.: Website attributes that increase consumer purchase intention: a conjoint analysis. J. Bus. Res. **63**(9), 1007–1014 (2010). https://doi.org/10.1016/j.jbusres.2009.01.023
12. Kesh, S., Ramanujan, S., Nerur, S.: A framework for analyzing e-commerce security. Inf. Manag. Comput. Secur. **10**(4), 149–158 (2002). https://doi.org/10.1108/09685220210436930

13. O'Gorman, L.: comparing passwords, tokens, and biometrics for user authentication. Proc. IEEE **91**(12), 2021–2040 (2003). https://doi.org/10.1109/JPROC.2003.819611

14. Nag, A.K., Roy, A., Dasgupta, D.: An adaptive approach towards the selection of multi-factor authentication. In: 2015 IEEE Symposium Series on Computational Intelligence, pp. 463–472 (2015). https://doi.org/10.1109/SSCI.2015.75

15. Lamport, L.: Password authentication with insecure communication. Commun. ACM **24**(11), 770–772 (1981)

16. Furnell, S.: An assessment of website password practices. Comput. Secur. **26**(7–8), 445–451 (2007). https://doi.org/10.1016/j.cose.2007.09.001

17. Furnell, S., Khern-am-nuai, W., Esmael, R., Yang, W., Li, N.: Enhancing security behaviour by supporting the user. Comput. Secur. **75**, 1–9 (2018). https://doi.org/10.1016/j.cose.2018.01.016

18. Albayram, Y., Khan, M.M.H., Fagan, M.: A study on designing video tutorials for promoting security features: a case study in the context of two-factor authentication (2FA). Int. J. Hum.-Comput. Interact. **33**(11), 927–942 (2017). https://doi.org/10.1080/10447318.2017.1306765

19. Colnago, J., Devlin, S., Oates, M., Swoopes, C., Bauer, L., Cranor, L., Christin, N.: "It's Not Actually That Horrible": exploring adoption of two-factor authentication at a university. In: Proceedings of the 2018 CHI Conference on Human Factors in Computing Systems, pp. 456:1–456:11. ACM, New York (2018). https://doi.org/10.1145/3173574.3174030

20. Furnell, S.: Assessing website password practices – over a decade of progress? Comput. Fraud Secur. **2018**(7), 6–13 (2018). https://doi.org/10.1016/S1361-3723(18)30063-0

21. Yu, J., Wang, G., Mu, Y., Gao, W.: An efficient generic framework for three-factor authentication with provably secure instantiation. IEEE Trans. Inf. Forensics Secur. **9**(12), 2302–2313 (2014). https://doi.org/10.1109/TIFS.2014.2362979

22. Furnell, S., Esmael, R.: Evaluating the effect of guidance and feedback upon password compliance. Comput. Fraud Secur. **2017**(1), 5–10 (2017). https://doi.org/10.1016/S1361-3723(17)30005-2

23. Saunders, M., Lewis, P., Thornhill, A.: Research Methods for Business Students (Seventh Ed). Pearson (2016)

24. Afrihost Answers. https://answers.afrihost.com/16427/received-following-notice-afrihost-requested-afrihost-account. Accessed 28 July 2020

25. Afrihost Answers. https://answers.afrihost.com/17429/cannot-verify-clientzone-because-cellphone-network-signal. Accessed 28 July 2020

Author Index

Ahmad, Atif   81
Aldabbas, Mohammad   20
Alshaikh, Moneer   81

Botha, Reinhardt A.   96
Bradshaw, Karen   129
Brandreth, Deen   144

da Veiga, Adéle   65

Jordaan, Jason   129

Langerman, Josef   1

Maynard, Sean B.   81
Mejri, Mohamed   34
Moganedi, Sophia   112

Nguyen, Minh   20

Ophoff, Jacques   144

Pilkington, Colin   50
Pottas, Dalenca   112

Singh, Mitesh   50
Solms, Rossouw Von   96

Teufel, Bernd   20
Teufel, Stephanie   20

van Rensburg, Ebenhaeser Otto Janse   96
van Staden, Wynand   50
von Solms, Johan   1

Yermalovich, Pavel   34

Printed in the United States
By Bookmasters